KNOWLEDGE AND SOCIAL IMAGERY

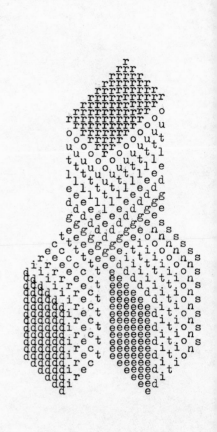

KNOWLEDGE AND SOCIAL IMAGERY

DAVID BLOOR

ROUTLEDGE DIRECT EDITIONS

ROUTLEDGE & KEGAN PAUL
London, Henley and Boston

First published in 1976
by Routledge & Kegan Paul Ltd
39 Store Street,
London WC1E 7DD,
Broadway House,
Newtown Road,
Henley-on-Thames,
Oxon RG9 1EN and
9 Park Street,
Boston, Mass. 02108, USA
Manuscript typed by A. Merrick
Printed and bound in Great Britain
by Unwin Brothers Limited,
The Gresham Press, Old Woking, Surrey
A member of the Staples Printing Group
© David Bloor 1976
ISBN 0 7100 8377 7

For Max Bloor

CONTENTS

PREFACE

In this book I discuss a number of problems which are vivid and immediate to us, although they sound abstract when formulated generally. They concern knowledge, particularly scientific knowledge. I am interested in what idea we form of these things when we reflect on them - for somehow we do manage to picture them to ourselves and these pictures can be powerful and influential. They are part of our self-awareness as members of a scientific culture. Indeed for those who are scientists these ideas are an even more intimate part of life, though in some way they touch us all.

I approach the problem from a very simple starting-point. If we want an account of the nature of scientific knowledge, surely, we can do no better than to adopt the scientific method itself. Science is a social phenomenon so we should turn to the sociologist of knowledge. The peculiar thing is that this immediately generates opposition from both sociologists and philosophers. They appear to have a ready-made conception of knowledge which precludes this simple course of action, claiming that it is foredoomed. Something odd and interesting is clearly going on. Some nerve has been touched. This is what the book is about.

The path of the argument, which may be judged from the contents page, traverses what may variously be described as the philosophy of science, the philosophy of the social sciences and the sociology of knowledge. There is no denying it: the book is a hybrid. I suspect that it is intrinsic to the subject under discussion that it should despoil academic boundaries. For these boundaries contrive to keep some things well hidden.

ACKNOWLEDGMENTS

I am anxious to express my gratitude to a number of people who kindly read drafts and parts of the book while it was in preparation. These are Barry Barnes, Celia Bloor, David Edge, Donald MacKenzie, Martin Rudwick and Steven Shapin. In all cases I have greatly benefited from their comments and criticisms. My helpful critics have not always agreed with what I have said and so I must stress that they are in no way responsible for the final outcome. Perhaps I would have been wise to make more extensive alterations in the light of their comments than I sometimes did.

It is only right that I single out of this list one of my colleagues at the Science Studies Unit, Barry Barnes. This is in order to express the very special debt that I owe to his thinking and work. This is too pervasive to be conveyed in footnotes, but is nevertheless keenly felt. Similarly, rather than make repeated references to his book 'Scientific Knowledge and Sociological Theory' (1974) I hope that a general acknowledgment will suffice. Certainly, anyone interested in the stand-point to be developed in the present book will find its discussions of first-rate importance. Nevertheless, although our two books share a number of important premises they develop quite different themes and press the argument into quite different areas.

I am grateful to the Hutchinson Publishing Group Ltd for permission to use a diagram from p. 13 of Z.P. Dienes's 'The Power of Mathematics' (1964). I must also record my appreciation to the historians of science whose scholarship I have pillaged to provide myself with examples and illustrations. Frequently I must be using their work in a manner of which they would not approve.

Chapter 1

THE STRONG PROGRAMME IN THE SOCIOLOGY OF KNOWLEDGE

Can the sociology of knowledge investigate and explain the very content and nature of scientific knowledge? Many sociologists believe that it cannot. They say that knowledge as such, as distinct from the circumstances surrounding its production, is beyond their grasp. They voluntarily limit the scope of their own enquiries. I shall argue that this is a betrayal of their disciplinary standpoint. All knowledge, whether it be in the empirical sciences or even in mathematics, should be treated, through and through, as material for investigation. Such limitations as do exist for the sociologist consist in handing over material to allied sciences like psychology or in depending on the researches of specialists in other disciplines. There are no limitations which lie in the absolute or transcendent character of scientific knowledge itself, or in the special nature of rationality, validity, truth or objectivity.

It might be expected that the natural tendency of a discipline such as the sociology of knowledge would be to expand and generalise itself: moving from studies of primitive cosmologies to that of our own culture. This is precisely the step that sociologists have been reluctant to take. Again, the sociology of knowledge might well have pressed more strongly into the area currently occupied by philosophers, who have been allowed to take upon themselves the task of defining the nature of knowledge. In fact sociologists have been only too eager to limit their concern with science to its institutional framework and external factors relating to its rate of growth or direction. This leaves untouched the nature of the knowledge thus created (cf. Ben-David (1971), DeGré (1967), Merton (1964) and Stark (1958)).

What is the cause for this hesitation and pessimism? Is it the enormous intellectual and practical difficulties which would attend such a programme? Certainly these must not be underestimated. A measure of their extent can be gained from the effort that has been expended on the more limited aims. But these are not the reasons that are in fact advanced. Is the sociologist at a loss for theories and methods with which to handle scientific knowledge? Surely not. His own discipline provides him with exemplary studies of the knowledge of other cultures which could be used as models and sources of inspiration. Durkheim's classic study 'The Elementary Forms of the Religious Life' shows how a sociologist can penetrate to the very depths of a form of knowledge. What is more Durkheim dropped a number of hints as to how his findings might relate to the study of scientific knowledge. The hints have fallen on deaf ears.

The cause of the hesitation to bring science within the scope of a thorough-going sociological scrutiny is lack of nerve and will. It is believed to be a foredoomed enterprise. Of course, the failure of nerve has deeper roots than this purely psychological characterisation suggests, and these will be investigated later. Whatever the cause of the malady, its symptoms take the form of a priori and philosophical argumentation. By these means sociologists express their conviction that science is a special case, and that contradictions and absurdities would befall them if they ignored this fact. Naturally philosophers are only too eager to encourage this act of self-abnegation (e.g. Lakatos (1971), Popper (1966)).

It will be the purpose of this book to combat these arguments and inhibitions. For this reason the discussions which follow will sometimes, though not always, have to be methodological rather than substantive. But hopefully they will be positive in their effect. Their aim is to put weapons in the hands of those engaged in constructive work to help them attack critics, doubters and sceptics.

I shall first spell out what I call the strong programme in the sociology of knowledge. This will provide the framework within which detailed objections will then be considered. Since a priori arguments are always embedded in background assumptions and attitudes it will be necessary to bring these to the surface for examination as well. This will be the second major topic and it is here that substantial sociological hypotheses about our conception of science will begin to emerge. The third major topic will concern what is perhaps the most difficult of all the obstacles to the sociology of knowledge, namely mathematics and logic. It will transpire that the problems of principle involved are not, in fact, unduly technical. I shall indicate how these subjects can be studied sociologically.

THE STRONG PROGRAMME

The sociologist is concerned with knowledge, including scientific knowledge, purely as a natural phenomenon. His definition of knowledge will therefore be rather different from that of either the layman or the philosopher. Instead of defining it as true belief, knowledge for the sociologist is whatever men take to be knowledge. It consists of those beliefs which men confidently hold to and live by. In particular the sociologist will be concerned with beliefs which are taken for granted or institutionalised, or invested with authority by groups of men.   Of course knowledge must be distinguished from mere belief.   This can be done by reserving the word 'knowledge' for what is collectively endorsed, leaving the individual and idiosyncratic to count as mere belief.

Men's ideas about the workings of the world have varied greatly. This has been true within science just as much as in other areas of culture.   Such variation forms the starting point for the sociology of knowledge and constitutes its main problem.   What are the causes of this variation, and how and why does it change?   The sociology of knowledge focuses on the distribution of belief and the various factors which influence it.   For example: how is knowledge transmitted; how stable is it; what processes go into its creation and maintenance; how is it organised and categorised into different disciplines or spheres?

For the sociologist these topics call for investigation and explanation and he will try to characterise knowledge in a way which accords with this perspective.   His ideas therefore will be in the same causal idiom as any other scientist.   His concern will be to locate the regularities and general principles or processes which appear to be at work within the field of his data.   His aim will be to build theories to explain these regularities.   If these theories are to satisfy the requirement of maximum generality they will have to apply to both true and false beliefs, and as far as possible the same type of explanation will have to apply in both cases.   The aim of physiology is to explain the organism in health and disease; the aim of mechanics is to understand machines which work and machines which fail; bridges which stand as well as those which fall. Similarly the sociologist seeks theories which explain the beliefs which are in fact found, regardless of how the investigator evaluates them.

Some typical problems in this area which have already yielded interesting findings may serve to illustrate this approach.   First, there have been studies of the connections between the gross social structure of groups and the general form of the cosmologies to which they have subscribed.   Anthropologists have found the social correlates, and the possible causes of men having anthropomorphic and magical world-views as distinct from impersonal and naturalistic one (Douglas (1966 and 1970)). Second, there have been studies which have traced the connections between economic, technical and industrial developments and the content of scientific theories.   For example, the impact of practical develop- ments in water and steam technology on the content of theories in thermo- dynamics has been studied in great detail.   The causal link is beyond dispute (Kuhn (1959), Cardwell (1971)).   Third, there is much evidence that features of culture which usually count as non-scientific greatly influence both the creation and the evaluation of scientific theories and findings.   Thus Eugenic concerns have been shown to underly and explain Francis Galton's creation of the concept of the coefficient of correlation in statistics.   Again the general political, social and ideological stand- point of the geneticist Bateson has been used to explain his role of sceptic in the controversy over the gene theory of inheritence (Coleman

(1970), Cowan (1972)).   Fourth, the importance that processes of training and socialisation have in the conduct of science is becoming increasingly documented.   Patterns of continuity and discontinuity, of
reception and rejection, appear to be explicable by appeal to these
processes.   An interesting example of the way in which a background in
the requirements of a scientific discipline influences the assessment of a
piece of work is afforded by Lord Kelvin's criticisms of the theory of
evolution.   Kelvin calculated the age of the sun by treating it as an in-
candescent body cooling down.   He found that it would have burnt itself
out before evolution could have reached its currently observable state.
The world is not old enough to have allowed evolution to have run its
course, so the theory of evolution must be wrong.   The assumption of
geological uniformity, with its promise of vast stretches of time, had been
rudely pulled from beneath the biologist's feet.   Kelvin's arguments
caused dismay.   Their authority was immense and in the 1860's they were
unanswerable; they followed with convincing rigour from convincing
physical premises.   By the last decade of the century the geologists had
plucked up courage to tell Kelvin that he must have made a mistake.   This
newfound courage was not because of any dramatic new discoveries, indeed,
there had been no real change in the evidence available.   What had
happened in the interim was a general consolidation in geology as a
discipline with a mounting quantity of detailed observation of the fossil
record.   It was this growth which caused a variation in the assessments
of probability and plausibility: Kelvin simply must have left some vital but
unknown factor out of consideration.   It was only with the understanding of
the sun's nuclear sources of energy that his physical argument could be
faulted.   Geologists and biologists had no foreknowledge of this, they
simply had not waited for an answer (Rudwick (1972), Burchfield (1975)).
This example also serves to make another point.   It deals with social
processes internal to science, so there is no question of sociological
considerations being confined to the operation of external influences.
      Finally, mention must be made of a fascinating and controversial
study of the physicists of Weimar Germany.   Forman (1971) uses their
academic addresses to show them taking up the dominant, anti-scientific
'Lebensphilosophie' surrounding them.   He argues 'that the movement to
dispense with causality in physics which sprang up so suddenly and
blossomed so luxuriantly in Germany after 1918, was primarily an effort
by German physicists to adapt the content of their science to the values of
their intellectual environment' (p.7).   The boldness and interest of this
claim derives from the central place of a-causality in modern quantum
theory.
      The approaches that have just been sketched suggest that the sociology
of scientific knowledge should adhere to the following four tenets.   In this
way it will embody the same values which are taken for granted in other
scientific disciplines.   These are:
      1 It would be causal, that is, concerned with the conditions which
         bring about belief or states of knowledge.   Naturally there will

be other types of causes apart from social ones which will co-operate in bringing about belief.

2 It would be impartial with respect to truth and falsity, rationality or irrationality, success or failure. Both sides of these dichotomies will require explanation.

3 It would be symmetrical in its style of explanation. The same types of cause would explain, say, true and false beliefs.

4 It would be reflexive. In principle its patterns of explanation would have to be applicable to sociology itself. Like the requirement of symmetry this is a response to the need to seek for general explanations. It is an obvious requirement of principle because otherwise sociology would be a standing refutation of its own theories.

These four tenets, of causality, impartiality, symmetry and reflexivity define what will be called the strong programme in the sociology of knowledge. They are by no means new, but represent an amalgam of the more optimistic and scientistic strains to be found in Durkheim (1938), Mannheim (1936) and Znaniecki (1965).

In what follows I shall try to maintain the viability of these tenets against criticism and misunderstanding. What is at stake is whether the strong programme can be pursued in a consistent and plausible way. Let us therefore turn to the main objections to the sociology of knowledge to draw out the full significance of the tenets and to see how the strong programme stands up to criticism.

THE AUTONOMY OF KNOWLEDGE

One important set of objections to the sociology of knowledge derives from the conviction that some beliefs do not stand in need of any explanation, or do not stand in need of a causal explanation. This feeling is particularly strong when the beliefs in question are taken to be true, rational, scientific or objective.

When men behave rationally or logically it is tempting to say that their actions are governed by the requirements of reasonableness or logic. The explanation of why a man draws the conclusion he does from a set of premises may appear to reside in the principles of logical inference themselves. Logic it may seem, constitutes a set of connections between premises and conclusions and men's minds can trace out these connections. As long as they are being reasonable then the connections themselves would seem to provide the best explanation for the beliefs of the reasoner. Like an engine on rails, the rails themselves dictate where it will go. It is as if men can transcend the directionless push and pull of physical causality and harness it, or subordinate it, to quite other principles and let these determine their thoughts. If this is so then it is not the sociologist or the psychologist but the logician who will provide the most important part of the explanation of belief.

Of course, when men make mistakes in their reasoning then logic itself is no explanation.   A lapse or deviation may be due to the inter- ference of a whole variety of factors.   Perhaps the reasoning is too difficult for the limited intelligence of the reasoner, perhaps he is in- attentive, or too emotionally involved in the subject under discussion. As when a train goes off the rails, a cause for the accident can surely be found.   But we neither have, nor need, commissions of enquiry into why accidents do not happen.

Arguments such as these have become a commonplace in contemp- orary analytical philosophy.   Thus in 'The Concept of Mind' (1949) Ryle says: ' Let the psychologist tell us why we are deceived; but we can tell ourselves and him why we are not deceived' (p.308).   This approach may be summed up by the claim that nothing makes people do things that are correct but something does make, or cause, them to go wrong (cf. Hamlyn (1969), Peters (1958)).

The general structure of these explanations stands out clearly. They all divide behaviour or belief into two types: right and wrong, true or false, rational or irrational.   They then invoke causes to explain the negative side of the division.   Causes explain error, limitation and deviation.   The positive side of the evaluative divide is quite different. Here logic, rationality and truth appear to be their own explanation. Here causes do not need to be invoked.

Applied to the field of intellectual activity these views have the effect of making a body of knowledge an autonomous realm.   Behaviour is to be explained by appeal to the procedures, results, methods and maxims of the activity itself.   It makes successful and conventional intellectual activity appear self-explanatory and self-propelling.   It becomes its own explanation.   No expertise in sociology or psychology is required: only expertise in the intellectual activity itself.

A currently fashionable version of this position is to be found in Lakatos's (1971) theory about how the history of science ought to be written.   This theory was explicitly meant to have implications for the sociology of science as well.   The first prerequisite, says Lakatos, is that a philosophy or methodology of science be chosen.   These are accounts of what science ought to be, and of what steps in it are rational. The chosen philosophy of science becomes the framework on which hangs all the subsequent work of explanation.   Guided by this philosophy it ought to be possible to display science as a process which exemplifies its principles and develops in accord with its teachings.   In as far as this can be done then science has been shown to be rational in the light of that philosophy.   This task, of showing that science embodies certain methodological principles, Lakatos calls either 'rational reconstruction' or 'internal history'.   For example, an inductivist methodology would perhaps stress the emergence of theories out of an accumulation of observations.   It would therefore focus on events like Kepler's use of Tycho Brahe's observations when formulating the laws of planetary motion.

It will never be possible, however, to capture all of the diversity of actual scientific practice by this means. Lakatos therefore insists that internal history will always need to be supplemented by an 'external history'. This looks after the irrational residue. It is a matter which the philosophical historian will hand over to the 'external historian' or the sociologist. Thus, from an inductivist standpoint the role of Kepler's mystical beliefs about the majesty of the sun would require a non-rational or external explanation.

The points to notice about this approach are first that internal history is self-sufficient and autonomous. To exhibit the rational character of a scientific development is sufficient explanation in itself of why the events took place. Second, not only are rational reconstructions autonomous; they also have an important priority over external history or sociology. The latter merely close the gap between rationality and actuality. This task is not even defined until internal history has had its say. Thus:

internal history is primary, external history only secondary, since the most important problems of external history are defined by internal history. External history either provides non-rational explanation of the speed, locality, selectiveness etc. of historical events as interpreted in terms of internal history; or when history differs from its rational reconstruction, it provides an empirical explanation of why it differs. But the rational aspect of scientific growth is fully accounted for by one's logic of scientific discovery (1971, p. 9).

Lakatos then answers the question of how to decide which philosophy should dictate the problems of external history or sociology. Alas for the externalist the answer represents yet a further humiliation. Not only is his function derivative; it now transpires that the best philosophy of science, according to Lakatos, is one which minimises his role. Progress in philosophy of science is to be measured by the amount of actual history which can be exhibited as rational. The better the guiding methodology the more of actual science is rendered safe from the indignity of empirical explanation. The sociologist is allowed a crumb of comfort from the fact that Lakatos is only too pleased to grant that there will always be some irrational events in science that no philosophy will ever be able or willing to rescue. He instances here unsavoury episodes of Stalinist intervention in science like the Lysenko affair in biology.

These refinements however are less important than the general structure of the position. It does not matter how the central principles of rationality are chosen, or how they might change. The central point is that, once chosen, the rational aspects of science are held to be self-moving and self-explanatory. Empirical or sociological explanations are confined to the irrational.

What can it mean to say that nothing makes people do or believe things which are rational or correct? Why in that case does the behaviour take place at all? What prompts the internal and correct functioning of an intellectual activity if the search for causes is only deemed appropriate in

the case of irrationality or error?   The theory that tacitly underlies these
ideas is a goal-directed or teleological vision of knowledge and rationality.

Suppose that it is assumed that truth, rationality and validity are
man's natural goal and the direction of certain natural tendencies with
which he is endowed.   Man is a rational animal and he naturally reasons
justly and cleaves to the truth when it comes within his view.   Beliefs
that are true clearly require no special comment.   For them, their truth
is all the explanation that is needed of why they are believed.   On the
other hand this self-propelling progress towards truth may be impeded or
deflected and here natural causes must be located.   These will account
for ignorance, error, confused reasoning and any impediment to
scientific progress.

Such a theory makes a great deal of sense of what is written in this
area even if it seems implausible at first sight to impute it to contemporary thinkers.   It even appears to have intruded itself into the thinking
of Karl Mannheim.   Despite his determination to set up causal and
symmetrical canons of explanation, his nerve failed him when it came to
such apparently autonomous subjects as mathematics and natural science.
This failure expressed itself in passages such as the following, from
'Ideology and Utopia'

> The existential determination of thought may be regarded as a
> demonstrated fact in those realms of thought in which we can show...
> that the process of knowing does not actually develop historically in
> accordance with immanent laws, that it does not follow   only from
> the 'nature of things' or from 'pure logical possibilities', and that
> it is not driven by an 'inner dialectic'.   On the contrary, the
> emergence and the crystallization of actual thought is influenced
> in many decisive points by extra-theoretical factors of the most
> diverse sort (1936, p.239).

Here social causes are being equated with 'extra-theoretical' factors.
But where does this leave behaviour conducted in accord with the inner
logic of a theory or governed by theoretical factors?   Clearly it is in
danger of being excluded from sociological explanation because it
functions as the base-line for locating those things which do require
explanation.   It is as if Mannheim slipped into sharing the sentiments
expressed in the quotations from Ryle and Lakatos and said to himself,
'When men do what is logical and proceed correctly, nothing more needs
to be said.'   But to see certain sorts of behaviour as unproblematic is to
see them as natural.   In this case what is natural is proceeding correctly,
that is via or towards the truth.   So here too the teleological model is
probably at work.

How does this model of knowledge relate to the tenets of the strong
programme?   Clearly it violates them in a number of serious ways.   It
relinquishes a thorough-going causal orientation.   Causes can only be
located for error.   Thus the sociology of knowledge is confined to the
sociology of error.   In addition it violates the requirements of symmetry
and impartiality.   A prior evaluation of the truth or rationality of a belief

is called for before it can be decided whether it is to be counted as self-explanatory or whether a causal theory is needed.   There is no doubt that if the teleological model is true then the strong programme is false.

The teleological and causal models, then, represent programmatic alternatives which quite exclude one another.   Indeed, they are two opposed metaphysical standpoints.   This may make it appear that it is necessary to decide at the outset which is true.   Doesn't the sociology of knowledge depend on the teleological view being false?   So doesn't this have to be established before the strong programme dare proceed?   The answer is 'no'.   It is more sensible to look at matters the other way round.   It is unlikely that any decisive, independent grounds could be adduced 'a priori' to prove the truth or falsity of such major metaphysical alternatives.   Where objections and arguments are proposed against one of the two theories it will be found that they depend on and presuppose the other, and so beg the question at issue.   All that can be done is to check the internal consistency of the different theories and then see what happens when practical research and theorising is based upon them.   If their truth can be decided at all it will only be after they have been adopted and used, not before.   So the sociology of knowledge is not bound to eliminate a rival standpoint.   It only has to separate itself from it, reject it, and make sure that its own house is in logical order.

These objections to the strong programme are thus not based on the intrinsic nature of knowledge but only on knowledge viewed from the standpoint of the teleological model.   Reject that model and all its associated distinctions, evaluations and asymmetries go with it.   It is only if that model has a unique claim to attention that its corresponding patterns of explanation are binding upon us.   Its mere existence, and the fact that some thinkers find it natural to use it, do not endow it with probative force.

In its own terms the teleological model is no doubt perfectly consistent and there are perhaps no logical reasons why anyone should prefer the causal approach to the goal-directed view.   There are, however, methodological considerations which may influence the choice in favour of the strong programme.

If explanation is allowed to hinge on prior evaluations then the causal processes that are thought to operate in the world will come to reflect the pattern of these evaluations.   Causal processes will be made to etch out the pattern of perceived error, throwing into relief the shape of truth and rationality.   Nature will take on a moral significance, endorsing and embodying truth and right.   Those who indulge their tendencies to offer asymmetrical explanations will thus have every opportunity to represent as natural what they take for granted.   It is an ideal recipe for turning one's gaze away from one's own society, values and beliefs and attending only to deviations from them.

Care is needed not to overstate this point, for the strong programme does exactly the same thing in certain respects.   It is also based on values, for example: the desire for generality of a specific kind and for a conception of the natural world as morally empty and neutral. So it too insists on giving nature a certain role with respect to morality, albeit of a negative kind. This means that it too represents as natural what it takes for granted.

What may be said, however, is that the strong programme possesses a certain kind of moral neutrality, namely the same kind as we have learned to associate with all the other sciences. It also imposes on itself the need for the same kind of generality as other sciences. It would be a betrayal of these values, of the approach of empirical science, to choose to adopt the teleological view. Obviously these are not reasons which could compel anyone to adopt the causal view. For some they may be precisely the reasons that would incline them to reject causality and adopt asymmetrical, teleological conceptions. But these points do make clear the ramifications of the choice and expose those values that are going to inform the approach to knowledge. From this type of confrontation, then, the sociology of knowledge can proceed, if it so chooses, without let or hinderance.

THE ARGUMENT FROM EMPIRICISM

The premise underlying the teleological model was that all causality is associated with error or limitation. This represents an extreme form of asymmetry and so stands as the most radical alternative to the strong programme with its insistence on symmetrical styles of explanation. It may be, however, that the strong programme can be criticised from a less extreme standpoint. Instead of all causation being associated with error is it not more plausible to say that some causes bring about erroneous belief whilst others bring about true belief? If it further transpires that certain types of cause are systematically correlated with true and false belief, respectively, then here is another basis for rejecting the symmetrical standpoint of the strong programme.

Consider the following theory: social influences produce distortions in our beliefs whilst the uninhibited use of our faculties of perception and our sensory-motor apparatus produce true beliefs. This praise for experience as a source of knowledge can be seen as encouraging the individual to rely on his own physical and psychological resources for getting to know the world. It is a statement of faith in the power of man's animal capacities for knowledge. Give these full play and their natural, but causal, operation will yield knowledge tested and tried in practical interaction with the world. Depart from this path, rely on one's fellow men, and one will be prey to superstitious stories, myth and speculation. At best these stories will be second-hand belief rather than first-hand knowledge. At worst the motives behind them will be corrupt, the product of liars and tyrants.

It is not difficult to recognise this picture. It is a version of Bacon's warning to avoid the Idols of the Tribe, the Market Place and the Theatre. Much of standard empiricism represents a refined and rarified statement of this approach to knowledge. Although the current fashion amongst empiricist philosophers is to avoid the psychological rendering of their theory the basic vision is not too dissimilar to that sketched above. I shall therefore refer to the above theory without more ado as empiricism.

If empiricism is correct then once again the sociology of knowledge is really the sociology of error, belief or opinion, but not knowledge as such. This conclusion is not as extreme as that derived from the teleological model of knowledge. It amounts to a division of labour between the psychologist and sociologist where the former would deal with real knowledge, the latter with error. The total enterprise would nevertheless be naturalistic and causal. There is therefore no question, as there was with the teleological model, of being confronted with a choice between a scientific perspective and a standpoint which embodies quite different values. Here the battle has to be fought entirely within science's own territory. Is the boundary between truth and error correctly drawn by this empiricist conception of knowledge? There are two shortcomings in empiricism which suggest that it is not.

First, it would be wrong to assume that the natural workings of man's animal resources always produce knowledge. They produce a mixture of knowledge and error with equal naturalness, and through the operation of one and the same type of cause. For example, a medium level of anxiety will often increase the learning and successful performance of a task compared with a very low level, but the performance will then drop again if the anxiety level gets too high. As a laboratory phenomenon the point is fairly general. A certain level of hunger will facilitate an animal's retention of information about his environment, as in a rat's learning of a laboratory maze for food. A very high level of hunger may well produce urgent and successful learning of the whereabouts of food, but it will lower the natural ability to pick up cues which are irrelevant to the current, overriding concern. These examples suggest that different causal conditions may indeed be associated with different patterns of true and false belief. However, they do not show that different types of cause correlate simply with true and false belief. In particular they show that it is incorrect to put psychological causes all on one side of this divide, as naturally leading to truth.

No doubt this shortcoming could be corrected. Perhaps all that the counter-examples show is that psychological learning machanisms have an optimum working arrangement and that they produce error when they are thrown out of focus. It may be insisted that when they are properly in focus then they have a potential for producing knowledge possessed by no other source. This revision of the doctrine may be granted because there is a far more important objection to it to be considered.

The crucial point about empiricism is its individualistic character. Those aspects of knowledge which each man can and has to furnish for himself may be adequately explained by this type of model.   But how much of man's knowledge, and how much of his science is built up by the individual relying simply on the interaction of the world with his animal capacities?   Probably very little.   The important question is: what analysis is to be given to the remainder?   It is plausible to say that the psychological approach leaves out of account the social component of knowledge.

Does not individual experience, as a matter of fact, take place within a framework of assumptions, standards, purposes and meanings which are shared?   Society furnishes the mind of the individual with these things and also provides the conditions whereby they can be sustained and reinforced.   If the individual's grasp of them wavers, there are agencies ready to remind him; if his view of the world begins to deviate there are mechanisms which encourage realignment.   The necessities of communication help to sustain collective patterns of thought in the individual psyche.   As well as the individual's sensory experience of the natural world,there is, then, something that points beyond that experience, that provides a framework for it and gives it a wider significance.   It fills out the individual's sense of what that over-all Reality is, that his experience is experience of.

The knowledge of a society designates not so much the sensory experience of its individual members, or the sum of what may be called their animal knowledge.   It is rather, their collective vision or visions of Reality.   Thus the knowledge of our culture, as it is represented in our science, is not knowledge of a reality that any individual can experience or learn about for himself.   It is what our best attested theories, and our most informed thoughts tell us is the case, despite what the appearances may say.   It is a story woven out of the hints and glimpses that we believe our experiments offer us.   Knowledge then, is better equated with Culture than Experience.

If this designation of the word 'knowledge' is accepted then the distinction between truth and error is not the same as the distinction between (optimum) individual experience and social influence.   Rather it becomes a distinction within the amalgam of experiences and socially mediated beliefs that make up the content of a culture.   It is a dis-crimination between rival mixtures of experience and belief.   The same two ingredients occur in true and false beliefs and so the way is open for symmetrical styles of explanation which invoke the same types of cause.

One way of putting this point which may assist its recognition and acceptance is to say that what we count as scientific knowledge is largely 'theoretical'.   It is largely a theoretical vision of the world that, at any given time, scientists may be said to know.   It is largely to their theories that scientists must repair when asked what they can tell us about the world.   But theories and theoretical knowledge are not things which are given in our experience.   They are what give meaning to experience by offering a story about what underlies, connects and accounts for it.   This does not mean that theory is unresponsive to

experience.   It is, but it is not given along with the experience it
explains, nor is it uniquely supported by it.   Another agency apart
from the physical world is required to guide and support this component
of knowledge.   The theoretical component of knowledge is a social
component, and it is a necessary part of truth, not a sign of mere error.
    Two major sources of opposition to the sociology of knowledge
have now been discussed and both have been rejected.   The teleological
model was indeed a radical alternative to the strong programme but
there is not the slightest compulsion to accept it.   The empiricist
theory is implausible as a description of what men in fact count as their
knowledge.   It provides some of the bricks but is silent on the designs
of the varying edifices that men build with them.   The next step will be
to relate these two positions to what is perhaps the most typical of all
objections to the sociology of knowledge.   This is the claim that it is
a self-refuting form of relativism.

THE ARGUMENT FROM SELF-REFUTATION

If someone's beliefs are totally caused and if there is necessarily
within them a component provided by society then it has seemed to many
critics that these beliefs are bound to be false.   Any thorough-going
sociological theory of belief then appears to be caught in a trap.   For
is not the sociologist bound to admit that his own thoughts are determined,
and in part even socially determined?   Must he not therefore admit that
his own claims are false in proportion to the strength of this
determination?   The result appears to be that no sociological theory
can be general in its scope otherwise it would reflexively enmesh itself
in error.   The sociology of knowledge is thus itself false or it must
make exceptions for scientific or objective investigations and hence
confine itself to the sociology of error.   There can be no self-consistent,
causal and general sociology of knowledge, especially not scientific
knowledge.
    It can be seen at once that this argument depends on one or the
other of the two conceptions of knowledge discussed above, namely the
teleological model or a form of individualistic empiricism.   The
conclusion follows, and it only follows, if these theories are first
granted.   This is because the argument takes as its premise their
central idea that causation implies error, deviation or limitation.   This
premise may be in the extreme form that any causation implies error or
in the weaker form that only social causation implies error.   One or the
other is crucial for the argument.
    These premises have been responsible for a plethora of feeble and
badly argued attacks on the sociology of knowledge.   Mostly the attacks
have failed to make explicit the premises on which they rest.   If they
had, their weakness would have been more easily exposed.   Their
apparent strength has derived from the fact that their real basis was

hidden or simply unknown.   Here is an example of one of the much
better forms of this argument which does make quite clear the standpoint from which it derives.

Grünwald, an early critic of Mannheim, is explicit in his
statement of the assumption that social determination is bound to
enmesh a thinker in error.   In the introduction to Mannheim's 'Essays
on the Sociology of Knowledge' (1952) Grünwald is quoted as saying:
'it is impossible to make any meaningful statement about the existential
determination of ideas without having any Archimedean point beyond all
existential determination...' (p.29).   Grünwald goes on to draw the
conclusion that any theory, such as Mannheim's, which suggests that
all thought is subject to social determination must refute itself.   Thus:
'No long argument is needed to show beyond doubt that this version of
sociologism, too, is a form of scepticism and therefore refutes itself.
For the thesis that all thinking is existentially determined and cannot
claim to be true claims itself to be true' (p. 29).

This would be a cogent objection against any theory that did indeed
assert that existential determination implied falsity.   But its premise
should be challenged for what it is: a gratuitous assumption and an unrealistic demand.   If knowledge does depend on a vantage point outside
society and if truth does depend on stepping above the causal nexus of
social relations, then we may give them up as lost.

There are a variety of other forms of this argument.   One typical
version is to observe that research into the causation of belief is itself
offered to the world as being correct and objective.   Therefore, the
argument goes, the sociologist assumes that objective knowledge is
possible, so not everybody's beliefs can be socially determined.   As
the historian Lovejoy (1940) put it: 'Even they, then, necessarily presuppose possible limitations or exceptions to their generalisations in
the act of defending them' (p.18).   The limitations the 'sociological
relativists' are said necessarily to presuppose are designed to make
room for criteria of factual truth and valid inference.   So this objection,
too, depends on the premise that factual truth and valid inference would
be violated by beliefs that are determined, or at least socially
determined.

Because these arguments have become so taken for granted their
formulation has become abbreviated and routine.   They can now be
given in such condensed versions as the following, provided by
Bottomore (1956): 'For if all propositions are existentially determined
and no proposition is absolutely true, then this proposition itself, if
true, is not absolutely true, but is existentially determined' (p.52).

The premise, that causation implies error on which all these
arguments depend have been exposed and rejected.   The arguments can
therefore be disposed of along with them.   Whether a belief is to be
judged true or false has nothing to do with whether it has a cause.

THE ARGUMENT FROM FUTURE KNOWLEDGE

Social determinism and historical determinism are closely related
ideas. Those who believe there are laws governing social processes
and societies will wonder if there are also laws governing their
historical succession and development. To believe that ideas are
determined by social milieu is but one form of believing that they are,
in some sense, relative to the actor's historical position. It is therefore not surprising that the sociology of knowledge has been criticised
by those who believe that the very idea of historical laws is based on
error and confusion. One such critic is Karl Popper (1960). It will be
the purpose of this section to refute these criticisms as far as they may
be applied to the sociology of knowledge.

The reason why the search for laws is held to be wrong is that if
they could be found they would imply the possibility of prediction. A
sociology which furnished laws could permit the prediction of future
beliefs. In principle it would seem to be possible, to know what the
physics of the future would be like just as it is possible to predict future
states of a mechanical system. If the laws of the mechanism are known
along with a knowledge of its initial position, and the masses and forces
on its parts, then all the future positions may be predicted.

Popper's objection to this ambition is partly informal and partly
formal. He informally observes that human behaviour and society just
do not furnish the same spectacle of repeated cycles of events as do some
limited portions of the natural world. So long-term predictions are
hardly realistic. This much may be certainly granted.

The nub of the argument, however, is a logical point about the
nature of knowledge. It is impossible, says Popper, to predict future
knowledge. The reason is that any such prediction would itself amount
to the discovery of that knowledge. The way men behave depends on
what they know so behaviour in the future will depend on this unpredictable knowledge and this too will be unpredictable. This argument
appears to depend on a peculiar property of knowledge and to result in a
gulf between the natural sciences and the social sciences in as far as
they dare to touch man as a knower. It suggests that the aspirations of
the strong programme with its search for causes and laws is misguided
and that something more modestly empirical is called for. Perhaps
sociology should again restrict itself to no more than a chronicle of errors
or a catalogue of external circumstances which help or hinder science.

In fact the point which Popper makes is a correct though trite one
which, properly understood, merely serves to emphasise the similarities
rather than the differences between the social and the natural sciences.
Consider the following argument which moves along exactly the same
steps as Popper's but would, if correct, prove that the physical world is
unpredictable. This will jerk our critical faculties into action. The
argument is this: It is impossible to make predictions in physics which
utilise or refer to physical processes of which we have no knowledge.

But the course of the physical world will depend in part on the operation of these unknown factors. Therefore the physical world is unpredictable.

Naturally the objection will be raised that all that this proves is that our predictions will often be wrong, not that nature is unpredictable. Our predictions will be falsified in as far as they fail to take into account relevant facts that we did not know were involved. Exactly the same rejoinder can be made to the argument against historical laws. Really Popper is offering an inductive argument based on our record of ignorance and failure. All that it points to is that our historical and sociological predictions will usually be false. The reason for this is correctly located by Popper. It is that men's future actions will often be contingent on things which they will know, but which we do not know now, and of which we therefore take no account when we make the prediction. The correct conclusion to be drawn for the social sciences is that we are unlikely to make much headway predicting the behaviour and beliefs of others unless we know at least as much as they do about their situation. There is nothing in the argument which need discourage the sociologist of knowledge from developing conjectural theories on the basis of empirical and historical case studies and testing them by further studies. Limited knowledge and the vast scope for error will ensure that these predictions will mostly be false. On the other hand the fact that social life depends on regularity and order gives grounds for hope that some progress will be possible. It is worth remembering that Popper himself sees science as an endless vista of refuted conjectures. Since this vision was not intended, and has not succeeded, in intimidating natural scientists there is no reason why it should appear in this light when it is applied to the social sciences - despite the fact that this is how Popper has chosen to present it.

But still the objection must be met: doesn't the social world present us with mere trends and tendencies and not the genuine law-like regularity of the natural world? Trends, of course, are merely contingent and superficial drifts rather than reliable necessities within phenomena. The answer is that this distinction is spurious. Take the orbiting planets, which are the usual symbols of law rather than trend. The solar system is a mere physical tendency. It endures because nothing disturbs it. There was a time when it did not exist and it is easy to imagine how it might be disrupted: a large gravitating body could pass close by it, or the sun could explode. Nor do the basic laws of nature even require the planets to move in ellipses. They only happen to orbit round the sun because of their conditions of origin and formation. Whilst obeying the same law of attraction their trajectories could be very different. No: the empirical surface of the natural world is dominated by tendencies. These tendencies wax and wane because of an underlying tustle of laws, conditions and contingencies. Our scientific understanding seeks to tease out those laws which, as we are prone to say, are 'behind' observable states of affairs. The contrast between the natural

and social worlds on which the objection depends fails to compare like
with like.   It compares the laws found to underly physical tendencies
with the purely empirical surface of social tendencies.

Interestingly, the word 'planet' originally meant 'wanderer'.
Planets attracted attention precisely because they did not conform to
the general tendencies visible in the night sky.   Kuhn's historical
study of astronomy, 'The Copernican Revolution' (1957), is a record of
just how difficult it is to find regularities beneath the tendencies.
Whether there are any underlying social laws is a matter for empirical
enquiry, not philosophical debate.   Who knows what wandering, aimless,
social phenomena will turn into symbols of law-like regularity?   The
laws that do emerge may well not govern massive historical tendencies,
for these are probably complex blends like the rest of nature.   The
law-like aspects of the social world will deal with the factors and
processes which combine to produce empirically observable effects.
Professor Mary Douglas's brilliant anthropological study 'Natural
Symbols' (1973) shows what such laws may look like.   The data is incomplete, her theories are still evolving, like all scientific works it is
provisional, but patterns can be glimpsed.

In order to bring the discussion of laws and predictions down to
earth it may be useful to conclude with an example.   This will show the
sort of law the sociologist of science actually looks for.   It will also
help to clarify the abstract terminology of 'law', and 'theory' which has
little practical currency in the conduct of either the sociology or
history of science.

The search for laws and theories in the sociology of science is
absolutely identical in its procedure with that of any other science.
This means that the following steps are to be found.   Empirical investigation will locate typical and recurrent events.   Such investigation
might itself have been prompted by some prior theory, the violation of
a tacit expectation or practical needs.   A theory must then be invented
to explain the empirical regularity.   This will formulate a general
principle or invoke a model to account for the facts.   In doing so it will
provide a language with which to talk about them and may sharpen
perception of the facts themselves.   The scope of the regularity may
be seen more clearly once an explanation of its first vague formulation
has been attempted.   The theory or model may, for example, explain
not only why the empirical regularity occurs but also why, sometimes,
it does not occur.   It may act as a guide to the conditions on which the
regularity depends and hence the causes for deviation and variation.
The theory, therefore, may prompt more refined empirical researches
which in turn may demand further theoretical work: the rejection of the
earlier theory or its modification and elaboration.

All of these steps may be seen in the following case.   It has often
been noted that priority disputes about discoveries are a common
feature of science.   There was a famous dispute between Newton and
Leibniz over the invention of the calculus; there was bitterness over

the discovery of the conservation of energy; Cavendish, Watt and
Lavoisier were involved in the dispute over the chemical composition
of water; biologists like Pasteur, medical men like Lister,
mathematicians like Gauss, physicists like Faraday and Davy all
became embroiled in priority disputes.   The approximately true
generalisation can thus be formulated: discoveries prompt priority
disputes.

It is quite possible to sweep this empirical observation aside and
declare it to be irrelevant to the true nature of science.   Science as
such, it may be said, develops according to the inner logic of scientific
enquiry and these disputes are mere lapses, mere psychological in-
trusions into rational procedures.   However a more naturalistic
approach would simply take the facts as they are and invent a theory to
explain them.   One theory which has been proposed to explain priority
disputes sees science as working by an exchange system. 'Contributions'
are exchanged for 'recognition' and status - hence all those eponymous
laws like Boyle's Law and Ohm's Law.   Because recognition is
important and scarce there will be struggles for it, hence priority
disputes, (Merton (1957), Storer (1966)).   The question then arises of
why it is not obvious who has made a certain contribution: why is it
possible for the matter to become one of dispute at all?   Part of the
answer is that because science depends so much on published and
shared knowledge, a number of scientists are often in a position to
make similar steps.   The race will be a close one between near equals.
But second, and more important, is the fact that discoveries involve
more than empirical findings.   They involve questions of theoretical
interpretation and reinterpretation.   The changing meaning of
empirical results provides rich opportunities for misunderstanding and
misdescription.

The discovery of oxygen will illustrate these complexities
(Toulmin (1957)).   Priestley is frequently credited with the discovery
of oxygen, but this is not how he saw the matter.   For him the new gas
that he isolated was dephlogisticated air.   It was a substance intimately
connected with combustion processes as conceived in terms of the
phlogiston theory.   It required the rejection of that theory and its
replacement by Lavoisier's account of combustion before scientists saw
themselves as dealing with a gas called oxygen.   It is the theoretical
components of science which give men the terms in which they see their
own and other's actions.   Hence those descriptions of actions which are
involved in the imputation of a discovery are precisely the ones which
become problematic when important discoveries are taking place.

Now it should be possible to offer an account of why some
discoveries are less prone to create priority disputes than others.   The
original empirical generalisation can be refined.   This refinement,
however, will not be a simple or arbitrary limitation on the scope of
the generalisation.   Rather, it will take the form of a discrimination
between different types of discovery prompted by the above reflections

on the exchange theory.   This allows for an improved statement of
the empirical law: discoveries at times of theoretical change prompt
priority disputes; those at times of theoretical stability do not.

Naturally the matter does not rest here.   First, the refined
version of the law has to be checked to see if it is empirically plausible.
This, of course, means checking a prediction about the beliefs and
behaviour of scientists.   Second, another theory needs to be developed
to make sense of the new law.   There is no need to go into more detail
although the point may be made that a theory has been formulated which
performs this task.   It is provided by T.S. Kuhn in his paper The
Historical Structure of Scientific Discovery (1962a) and his book 'The
Structure of Scientific Revolutions' (1962).   More will be said about
this view of science in a subsequent chapter.

It does not matter for the present whether the exchange model, or
Kuhn's account of science, is correct.   What is at issue is the general
way in which empirical findings and theoretical models relate, interact
and develop.   The point is that they work here in exactly the same way
as they do in any other science.

Chapter 2

SENSE-EXPERIENCE, MATERIALISM AND TRUTH

The aim of this chapter will be to continue the examination of the strong programme by discussing in more detail the relation between the empirical and social components in knowledge. The purpose of the previous chapter was to go straight to the erroneous assumptions which underlay the objections to the strong programme. Here an attempt will be made to consolidate these conclusions by offering a more positive account. The brief discussion of empiricism needs to be supplemented, and something must be said about the notion of truth.

I shall begin by stressing the vital insights that empiricism affords the sociology of knowledge. There are great dangers in being aware of the shortcomings of empiricism without seeing its virtues. For the sociologist of science these dangers centre around the question of the reliability of sense perception and the correct theoretical analysis to be given to cases of misperception in science. Misperception has attracted the attention of sociologists because it offers a tempting avenue of approach to the operation of social factors in science. This is legitimate and valuable. But if sociologists make misperception a central feature of their analysis they may fail to come to terms with the reliability, repeatability and dependability of science's empirical basis. They will fail to allow for the role within science of experimental procedures, controls and practices. These guard against misperception, define it, expose it, and correct it. If sociologists are overly attracted to a bold and debunking stress on misperception they will soon pay the price. Their research will be confined to the sociology of error not to knowledge in general. They will have failed to do justice both to science and themselves. What, then, is the general theoretical significance of sensory unreliability for the sociology of knowledge? I shall first outline the more usual sociological analysis of misperception, and then counter-attack.

THE RELIABILITY OF SENSE-EXPERIENCE

Psychologists, historians and sociologists have provided fascinating
examples of social processes interacting with perception, or perception
and recall. Men are trained in certain ways and their interests and
expectations are endowed with a structure. Unexpected events then
take place before their eyes and are not seen - or if they are seen, they
evoke no response. No meaning is attached to the experiences and no
action prompted by them. Conversely, where some observers see
nothing, or detect no order and pattern in their experience, others do
have experiences, or recall having experiences, which fall into line with
their expectations.

For example, a number of geologists visited the parallel roads of
Glen Roy in Scotland. These are strange, horizontal, road-like
phenomena to be seen on the hillsides of Glen Roy. Darwin with his
experience aboard the 'Beagle' of earthquakes and rising beaches in
South America held the theory that the parallel roads were caused by the
sea. Agassiz, with his experience of glaciers in Switzerland had another
vision of their cause. The roads were the action of lakes dammed up by
ice during the ice-age. The different theories led to different expectations concerning the extent and position of the roads, and duly different
findings were reported by the different observers. Agassiz, whose
glacial theory later triumphed saw, or believed he had seen the roads,
where no one since has been able to discern them (Rudwick (1974)).

How are these events to be understood? Since many such cases
involve scientists not seeing things which contradict their theory one
approach has been to assimilate them to the phenomenon of 'resistance
to scientific discovery'. This is how Barber treats them when discussing a variety of cases in which the ideal of open-mindedness has been
violated by scientists (Barber (1961)). These cases include the
resistance to new ideas, theories and approaches; resistance to unusual
techniques like the use of mathematics in biology; as well as resistance
to interpretations that may be put on sensory experience.

In a case study Barber and Fox (1958) report how a biologist
followed up the accidental and unexpected discovery that intravenous
injections of an enzyme caused the ears of laboratory rabbits to go floppy.
Although the injections were originally given for quite another purpose
this surprising phenomenon naturally prompted the researcher to section
the ears and peer at them down a miscroscope to see what had caused the
effect. Against a background assumption, shared with other workers,
that the cartilage in the ears was an inert and uninteresting substance,
he concentrated attention on the connective and elastic tissue. The
cartilage was examined as well but, as was expected, did not appear to
be implicated, 'the cells were healthy-looking and there were nice nuclei.
I decided there was no damage to the cartilage. And that was that.'
The uniformly healthy appearance of the ear tissues was baffling. What
was the mechanism of the enzyme that had caused the very visible effect?

It was only some years later when other research was less pressing, and teaching material was required for seminars on experimental pathology, that the problem of the rabbits' ears was resurrected. This time the researcher prepared two sections of rabbit ears for the purpose of demonstration. Mindful of textbook procedure for research, one of these rabbits had been treated with the enzyme whilst the other was untreated. It then became obvious on inspection that the two microscope slides were different. The hitherto unsuspected cartilage had changed under treatment showing loss of the intercellular matrix, enlargement of the cells and a variety of other effects. The prior assumption that cartilage was inactive meant, as Barber put it, that the scientist 'had been blinded by his scientific preconceptions'.

Barber's overall theoretical interpretation is what is of interest and this will lead back to the question of how appropriate the reference to blindness is in this case. Barber argues that violations of the norm of open-mindedness are a constant feature of science. These violations have certain identifiable sources such as theoretical and methodological commitments, high professional standing, specialisation, and so forth. Certain features of science that are valuable or functional in some respects prove disfunctional in others.

Applied to perception this suggests that a certain quantity of misperception is a direct consequence of processes which expedite research. This idea, that misperception is in some sense normal, is a very valuable one. Let us firmly retain it.

Barber's analysis contains one discordant note. He says that misperception is a pathological phenomenon. Like a disease it needs to be understood so that it can be treated and removed. Some resistance is perhaps inevitable but hopefully its level may be progressively diminished. But can misperception be such a natural consequence of a functional and healthy aspect of science and at the same time be wished away? Surely it cannot. Barber's argument should have proceeded here with the same tough-minded logic as did Durkheim's famous discussion of crime in his 'Rules of Sociological Method' (1938). To try to remove crime would be to stifle valuable forces making for diversity and individuality. Impose enough pressure to remove what we now count as crimes and other activities will move to the front of the queue of threats to social order. The question is not whether to have crime, it is only a matter of which crimes. It is inevitable, roughly constant and necessary. It may be deplored but to desire that it be reduced without limit is to misunderstand how society works. The same should be said of misperception.

Such a conception is entirely consistent with the psychological literature on what are called signal-detection tasks. This is the problem of detecting a signal from a background of noise, for example a faint spot on a blurred radar screen. The tendency to decide that a signal has indeed been seen is related in a lawful way to the known consequences

of these decisions.   Whether subjects actually perceive a signal
depends on whether they know that it is important not to miss any
signal or whether it is vital never to give a false alarm.   Varying
these parameters produces different patterns of perception and misperception.   The important point is that the attempts to cut down the
number of false alarms inevitably leads to signals being missed.
Attempts never to miss a signal inevitably give rise to false alarms.
There is a trade-off between different sorts of misperception and this
is a function of the social matrix of consequences and meanings within
which the perception takes place.

Misperception, then, is indeed inevitable, roughly constant and
cannot be reduced without limit.   It is intimately connected with the
socio-psychological organisation of scientific activity.   It provides a
valuable indicator of them and a useful research tool.   It may be used
to detect the influence of factors like commitment, direction of interest,
differences of theoretical approach, and so forth.

This standpoint is a valuable one, but if it is easy to shrink from
some of its implications, as Barber did, it is equally easy to extra-
polate it in a thoughtless and self-defeating way.   To keep it in proper
focus consider some of its limitations.

First, the meaning of the historical examples and case studies
given above is not as straightforward as it may appear.   Are they
really cases of misperception, or may they not with equal plausibility
illustrate the weaknesses of quite a different psychological faculty,
namely, memory?   Had Agassiz and Darwin walked side by side along
Glen Roy it is difficult to believe that they would not have been able to
agree on what was before them.   Even if they had put different con-
structions on the meaning of the angle of a slope, the presence of
certain types of shell, boulder or sand they would surely have agreed
about what objects they were interpreting differently.   Was it Agassiz's
perception that was influenced by his theory or the simplifying,
amplifying process of remembering and interpreting in retrospect what
he had seen?

A similar point holds for the researcher looking down the microscope at the specimen of cartilage.   Did he see something different
when he looked at the isolated specimen than when he was able to
compare the treated and the untreated samples directly?   Although at
one point Barber talks in terms of scientists being blinded by their
preconceptions elsewhere he talks in terms of a failure of memory.   He
says that in the first case the researcher only had his memory image
to compare with his single microscope slide.   If the memory image
was weak or distorted this could account for the error of judgment that
allowed the scientist to pass over the evidence before his eyes.   (The
constructive character of memory was investigated from a socio-
psychological standpoint in Bartlett's classic 'Remembering' (1932)).

These points are not as pedantic as they may sound.   Their
significance is that any criticisms of sense-perception that rest on

examples such as these are equivocal and guilty of oversimplification.
They are likely to do less than justice to sense-perception. It is
perfectly consistent to maintain that sense-perception is reliable,
whilst acknowledging that the involvement of memory is ever likely to
show unreliability. Any experimental procedure which relies on the
decaying records of memory when direct evidence is available is
doubtful science.

Again, it could be rightly insisted that signal-detection
experiments do not really capture the circumstances in which scientific
observations are usually made. The whole point of proper
experimental design, the use of instruments and control groups, is to
avoid putting the observer in the position of having to make difficult
discriminations, or snap-judgments. Perhaps Agassiz was simply in
a hurry, but a good observer puts himself in as favourable a position
as possible to make his observations, judgments and comparisons.
They are recorded at the time they are made and not in retrospect; a
sample is matched with a control in such a way that memory does not
intervene; and so on. Given standardised conditions for observation
and the well-known precautions embedded in the lore of experimental
technique, then the deliverances of the senses can be relied upon to be
uniform from person to person and to be independent of theories and
commitments. When an experimental procedure does not produce
uniform results, or seems to produce different results for different
observers, then the design is deemed to be a bad one or the experiment
misconceived and unreliable.

To see the power of this common sense empiricism it is only
necessary to recall one of the most famous, or infamous, examples of
science which would fit the signal-detection model of perception. This
is the case of the discovery of N-rays in 1903 by Blondlot a French
physicist and member of the Academy of Sciences. Blondlot believed
that he had found a new form of ray rather like the X-rays that had
recently been the focus for much excited research.

His apparatus consisted of a hot platinum wire inside an iron tube
which had a small window in it. The N-rays, which could not pass
through the iron, came out of the window. The means of detecting the
rays was to let them fall on a very faintly illuminated screen in a
darkened room. The slight increase in intensity of the screen indicated the presence of the rays. Blondlot found that N-rays had a
variety of properties. Objects could store them; people could emit
them; and noise interfered with them. Even negative N-rays were
observed which, under certain conditions, decreased the illumination
of the screen (Langmuir (1953)).

The physicist R.W. Wood visited the French laboratories whilst
Blondlot was studying the refraction of N-rays through an aluminium
prism. By this time Blondlot had found that N-rays were not mono-
chromatic but were made up of a number of components with different
refractive indices. During the course of one of these experiments, and

unseen by Blondlot in the darkened laboratory, Wood removed the
prism from the apparatus. This should have stopped the experiment
but the unfortunate Blondlot proceded to detect on the screen the same
pattern of signals that he had been detecting before (see Wood (1904)).
Whatever was the cause of his experiences it was not N-rays.
Presumably this result, like the rest of the phenomena, was caused
by Blondlot's belief in the N-rays.

The trouble lay in Blondlot's experimental design. His
detection process was at the very threshold of sensation. When the
signal noise ratio is as unfavourable as this then subjective experience
is at the mercy of expectation and hope. The expected social consequences, the social 'pay-off matrix', become crucial variables.

The significant feature of the discovery of the spurious N-rays
is how rapidly and unanimously British, German and American
physicists realised that something was badly wrong with the
experimental reports (Watkins (1969). For an early physiological
theory of Blondlot's results see Lummer (1904)). What is more, it
was remarkably easy for Wood to demonstrate the error. He performed a simple, controlled experiment: take the readings with and
then without the prism and hence with and without the allegedly re-
fracted N-rays. The results are the same therefore the cause had
nothing to do with the rays. The lapse was a personal and psychological failure of competence by Blondlot and his compatriots. They
fell short of common and standardised procedures. It puts the
reliability of some Frenchmen in doubt, not the whole of perception.

Sociologists would be walking into a trap if they accumulated
cases like Blondlot's and made them the centre of their vision of
science. They would be underestimating the reliability and repeatability of its empirical base; it would be to remember only the
beginning of the Blondlot story and to forget how and why it ended.
The sociologist would be putting himself where his critics would, no
doubt, like to see him - lurking amongst the discarded refuse in
science's back yard.

The two lines of the argument can now be brought together.
Starting from case studies of theory-biased observation, the conclusion was that some misperception was inevitable. A dose of
empiricist common sense then reminded us that science has its
procedural norms for good experiment and that many cases of the
alleged unreliability of sense-perception were really due to cutting
scientific corners and the failure to observe due precautions. Naturally
these cases are transient, detectable and correctable. Fortunately
these two lines of argument are not in any way opposed to one another.

A steady stream of unavoidable misperceptions are always going
to take place at the margins of scientific concern. Science has to be
finite in its interests; it must have a boundary. Along that boundary
events and processes will necessarily receive scant and fluctuating
attention. Here the signal-detection analogy does apply. Events which

with hindsight can be seen to be significant will frequently be missed
or dismissed.

The situation changes at the centre of attention. Here a limited
number of empirical processes will be the focus of concern and debate.
The requirements of repeatability, reliability, good experimental
design, and the avoidance of threshold effects will be strictly enforced.
Errors will be avoidable and avoided. Where they are not avoided
sanctions will be applied either directly by others or through conscience -
the internalised image of reproach. Barber's scientist working on the
rabbits, who finally made his discovery when he used properly controlled
procedures, reported a feeling of shame, 'It still makes me writhe to
think of it'. More dramatically and sadly Blondlot's career was ruined.
Nothing could more vividly show the operation of social norms than
shame and ostracism.

What these case studies really show is not how unreliable
perception is, or that it is a function of men's desires, but how
compelling is the demand by science that its standardised procedures be
adhered to. These procedures declare that experience is admissible
only in as far as it is repeatable, public and impersonal. That it is
possible to locate experience that has this character is undeniable. That
knowledge should be deemed to be crucially linked to this facet of our
experience is, however, a social norm. It is a conventional and variable stress. Other activities and other forms of knowledge have other
norms which stress the evanescence, inwardness and individuality of
experience. It is also undeniable that some of our experience has this
character too, and it is worth remembering that science has not always
been hostile to these models (cf. French (1972) and Yates (1972)).

I shall now offer a brief positive characterisation of the role of
experience which shows how it is possible to do justice to its influence
on belief without diminishing the claims of the strong programme. This
will bring out the relation between the stress that has just been put on
the reliability of experience and the remarks made earlier about the inadequacy of an empiricist conception of knowledge.

EXPERIENCE AND BELIEF

The valuable insight of empiricism is its claim that our physiology
ensures that some responses to our material environment are common
and constant. These responses are called our perceptions. Cultural
variation is plausibly thought of as imposed on a stratum of biologically
stable sensory capacities. To work with the assumption that the
faculty of perception is relatively stable is no retreat from the view that
its deliverances do not, and cannot, in themselves, constitute knowledge.
This is because experience always impinges on a state of prior belief.
It is a cause which brings about an alteration of that state of belief. The
resulting state will always arise by compounding the fresh influence with

the old state of affairs.   This means that experience may bring about
change but does not uniquely determine the state of belief.

One way of holding this picture in mind is to draw an analogy
with the effect of a force impinging on a system of forces.   It will influence but not uniquely determine the resultant force.   Think here of
the parallelogram of forces.   The analogy is illustrated in Figure 1.

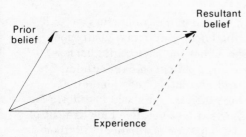

FIGURE 1

As the component which represents experience is made to vary so is
the resultant belief.   Clearly no value of the experience component
corresponds to a unique value of the resultant belief without first
fixing the state of the prior belief.   This always needs to be taken into
account when thinking about what effect an experience will have.   Nor
does any pattern or sequence of changing experiences in itself determine
a unique pattern of changing belief.   No wonder that simply observing
the world does not allow men to agree about what is the true account
that is to be given of it.

Consider the following simple example.   A primitive tribesman
consults an oracle by administering a herbal substance to a chicken.
The chicken dies.   The tribesman can clearly see its behaviour and so
can we.   He says the oracle has answered 'no' to his question.   We say
the chicken has been poisoned.   The same experience impinging on
different systems of belief evokes different responses.   This applies
both at the superficial level of what we might casually say about the
event and also at the deeper level of what we believe its meaning to be,
and how we would act subsequently.

Scientific examples of the same kind are easy enough to find.   The
most obvious is perhaps the different meanings which at different times
have been put on the daily movement of the sun.   The subjective
experience of the sun's movement is one in which the horizon acts as a
stable frame against which the movement appears to take place.   It
is plausible and testable to assume that this will be the same for all
observers.   What is believed about the actual relative positions of the
sun and the earth, however, is very different for followers of Ptolemy
and followers of Copernicus.

The social component in all this is clear and irreducible. Processes such as education and training must be invoked to explain the enplanting and the distributing of the states of prior belief. They are absolutely necessary if experience is to have a determinate effect. These processes are also necessary for an understanding of how the resultant beliefs are sustained and to account for the patterns of relevance that connect experiences to some beliefs rather than others. Although this view incorporates some of the insights of empiricism it entails that no belief falls outside the sociologist's purview. There is a social component in all knowledge.

Empiricism is currently out of favour in many quarters so is it not ill-advised to incorporate such a blatantly empiricist component into the sociology of knowledge? Should not the sociologist eschew views which have been subject to extensive philosophical criticism? If this means that the sociologist should resolutely keep himself at arm's length from philosophical fashion then it is a sound instinct. But if it means that he should fight shy of ideas just because they are out of favour with philosophers, then it is a recipe for cowardice. Rather, the sociologist and psychologist should exploit whatever ideas are of use to them and put upon them whatever construction suits the purposes in hand.

The version of empiricism that is here being incorporated into the sociology of knowledge is really a psychological theory. It says that our perceptual and thinking faculties are two different things and that our perceptions influence our thinking more than our thinking influences our perceptions. This form of empiricism makes biological and evolutionary sense but it is as much despised by modern empiricists as it is by the modern critics of empiricism. Contemporary philosophers have turned this psychological thesis about two faculties into a claim about the existence and nature of two different languages: the data language and the theoretical language. Or again, they talk of the status of two different sorts of belief: those that are immediately given by experience and are certainly true and those only indirectly connected with experience whose truth is problematic. These are the claims that are currently subject to philosophical debate. The absolute certainty, or even the high probability, of beliefs allegedly derived immediately from experience has been questioned, and more recently so has the whole conception of two different languages (Hesse (1974)).

Let these issues of justification, and of logic and language, be negotiated by philosophers how they will. All that matters for a naturalistic study of knowledge is that it has a plausible and substantial picture of the role of sensory experience. If this happens to be in the same idiom as an old-fashioned, psychological empiricism then so much the better for our philosophical heritage. It shows that it is being taken in the spirit in which it was offered (Bloor (1975)).

MATERIALISM AND SOCIOLOGICAL EXPLANATION

No consistent sociology could ever present knowledge as a fantasy un-
connected with men's experiences of the material world around him.
Men cannot live in a dream world.   For consider how such a fantasy
would have to be transmitted to new members of society.   It would
depend on education, training, indoctrination, social influence and
pressure.   All of these presuppose the reliability of perception and the
ability to detect, retain and act upon perceived regularities and discriminations.   Human bodies and voices are part of the material world
and social learning is part of learning how the material world functions.
If men have the equipment and the propensity to learn from one another
they must in principle have the ability to learn about the regularities of
the non-social world.   In all cultures they do precisely this in order to
survive.   If social learning can rely on the organs of perception then so
can natural or scientific knowledge.   No sociological account of science
can place the reliability of sense-perception any lower when it is used in
the laboratory or on the field trip then when it is used in social interaction or collective action.   The whole edifice of sociology presumes
that men can systematically respond to the world through their
experience, that is, through their causal interaction with it.   Materialism
and the reliability of sense experience are thus presupposed by the
sociology of knowledge and no retreat from these assumptions is
permissible.
      To illustrate the role of such factors consider the interesting
comparison made by J.B. Morrell (1972) of two early nineteenth-century
research schools.   Morrell compared Thomas Thomson's laboratory
at Glasgow with Justus Liebig's at Giessen.   Both men pioneered
university schools of practical chemistry during the 1820s.   Liebig's
flourished and became world famous.   Thomson's ultimately faded into
obscurity and left little mark on the history of the subject.   The problem
Morrell set himself was to compare and contrast the factors which
produced the markedly different fates of the schools despite their
similarity in so many respects.
      His analysis is conspicuously symmetrical and causal.   He proceeds
by setting up an 'ideal type' of a research school which incorporated all
the factors and parameters which bear upon their organisation and
success.   Once this model has been erected it then becomes clear how
different the cases of Glasgow and Giessen were, despite their common
structure.   The factors to be taken into account were the psychological
make-up of the director of the school; his financial resources and his
power and status in his university; his ability to attract students and what
he could offer them in terms of motivation and career; the reputation of
the director in the scientific community; his choice of field and research
programme and the techniques he had perfected for further research.
      Thomson was a possessive, sarcastic man who tended to treat the
products of his students' labours as if they were his own property.

Whilst of course acknowledging their contribution, they would be published in books under Thomson's own name.   Liebig could also be a difficult and aggressive man but he was venerated by his students. He encouraged them to publish work under their own names and controlled a journal which provided an outlet for this work.   He also offered his students the degree of Ph.D. and other help in their academic and industrial careers.   No such useful, rounded educational process was offered in Thomson's laboratory.

At first both directors had to finance the running of their school out of their own pockets.   Liebig was the more successful of the two in getting others to finance his laboratory, its materials and staff.   He was able to shift this burden on to the state, something that was quite unthinkable in laissez-faire Britain.   After some initial difficulty over his status Liebig established himself as a professor at a small university with no distractions from his main work.   Thomson was a Regius rather than a College professor at Glasgow and felt an outsider. He was burdened with teaching in the large medical school and dissipated his energy in university chores and politics.

The two directors made markedly different choices in the field of their research.   Thomson was quick to see the value and interest of Dalton's atomic theory and devoted himself to a programme of finding atomic weights and the chemical composition of salts and minerals. One of his major concerns was Prout's hypothesis: that all atomic weights are whole number multiples of the atomic weight of hydrogen. Thomson, then, went into inorganic chemistry. This was a well-worked field, and some of the best practitioners of the time, such as Berzelius and Gay-Lussac were well established in it.   Furthermore the techniques involved demanded the very highest skill, and the task of inorganic analysis was beset with many practical problems and complexities. It was difficult to achieve stable, repeatable and useful results.

Liebig chose the new field of organic chemistry.   He developed an apparatus and a technique of analysis capable of routinely producing reliable, repeatable findings.   Moreover the apparatus could be used by an average, competent and industrious student.   In short he was able to set up something like a factory, and it was a factory which produced what nobody in the area had produced before.

Thomson's findings and those of his students frequently ran into the problem that they differed from those of others, and their work was criticised by Berzelius.   The school's results sometimes contradicted one another and they were not seen as revealing or useful.   Thomson was convinced of the accuracy of his findings but to others they often appeared merely adventitious and unilluminating.   By contrast, nobody could gainsay Liebig and his students.

The crucial methodological issue in the present context is to decide what examples such as this say about the role of men's experience of the material world in sociological explanations of science.   I shall argue that taking into account the way the material world behaves does not interfere with either the symmetry or the causal character of sociological explanations.

There is no denying that part of the reason why Liebig was a success was because the material world responded with regularity when subject to the treatment given it in his apparatus. By contrast if anyone behaves towards the material world in the precise way in which Thomson did then no such regularity will appear. His procedures presumably cut across and tangled together the physical and chemical processes at work within the substances he examined. The pattern, both of human behaviour and the consequent feedback of experience, is different in the two cases.

The overall style of explanation of the fate of the two research schools is nevertheless identical in the two cases. Both cases have to be understood by reference to an 'input' from the world. Both cases start from the behavioural confrontation of the scientist with a selected part of his environment. In this sense and thus far the two explanations are symmetrical with one another. The account then went on, still quite symmetrically, to deal with the system of existing beliefs, standards, values and expectations on to which these results impinged. Clearly there are different causes at work in the two cases otherwise there would not be different effects. The symmetry resides in the types of causes.

The differences in laboratory findings is just part of the overall causal process which culminated in the different fate of the two schools. It is not in itself a sufficient explanation for these facts. It would not be adequate to say that the facts of chemistry explain why the one programme failed and other succeeded. Given exactly the same laboratory behaviour and the same experimental outcomes the fates of the two schools could have been the other way round. For example, suppose that nobody had been very interested in organic chemistry. Liebig's efforts would have been frustrated, just as the biologist Mendel was frustrated. He would have been ignored. Or conversely suppose that inorganic chemistry had not been so actively studied when Thomson set up his school. His contribution would have stood out more prominently. With the opportunities and encouragement that this higher status would have given, his school may have flourished and gone on to make very different and more lasting contributions. It too may have become a successful factory with reliable methods of production.

There is one situation in which it might be permissible to say that the chemistry alone was the cause of a difference, whether in belief, theory, judgment or, as in this case, the fate of two research schools. This would be where all the social, psychological, economic and political factors were identical, or only differed in minor or irrelevant ways. Even this situation would not really constitute any retreat from the strong programme. It would not make the sociological factors ir- relevant for the overall explanation. They would still be vitally active, but merely left unattended to for the moment because they are evenly balanced or 'controlled'.   The full structure of the explanation, even in these cases would be just as causal and symmetrical.

TRUTH, CORRESPONDENCE AND CONVENTION

Truth is a very prominent concept in our thinking but so far little has been said about it.   The strong programme enjoins sociologists to disregard it in the sense of treating both true and false beliefs alike for the purposes of explanation.   It may appear that the discussion in the last section violated this requirement.   Put bluntly, didn't Liebig's laboratory flourish because it really discovered truths about the world, and didn't Thomson's fail because of the errors in his findings?   The fate of these enterprises surely depended on matters of truth and falsity, so these appear to play a central role after all.   The link between truth and the strong programme must be clarified, especially for those parts of the programme which stress the causal promptings of the world as they appear in experimental results and sensory experiences.

There is little doubt about what we mean when we talk of truth. We mean that some belief, judgment or affirmation corresponds to reality and that it captures and portrays how things stand in the world. Talk of this kind is probably universal.   The need to reject what some men say, and affirm what others say, is basic to human interaction.   It may seem unfortunate, then, that this common conception of truth should be so very vague.   The relation of correspondence between knowledge and reality on which it hinges is difficult to characterise in an illuminating way.   A variety of words like 'fit', 'match', or 'picture' suggest them-selves, but one is hardly better than another.   Instead of trying to define the concept of truth more sharply a different approach will be adopted. This is to ask to what use the concept of truth is put and how the notion of correspondence functions in practice.   It will transpire that the vagueness of the concept of truth is neither surprising nor any hardship.

To make the issue tangible consider again the example of the phlogiston theory.   Phlogiston was tentatively identified with the gas we call hydrogen.   The chemists of the eighteenth century knew how to pre-pare this gas but their conception of its properties and behaviour was very different to ours.   They believed, for example, that phlogiston would be absorbed by a substance they called 'minium'   or 'lead calx' - or what we would call 'lead oxide'.   Furthermore they believed that when it absorbed phlogiston the minium would turn into lead (cf. Conant (1966)).

Joseph Priestley was able to provide a convincing demonstration of this theory.   He took an inverted gas jar filled with phlogiston which was trapped over water (see Figure 2).   Floating on the water was a crucible containing some minium.   This was heated by using the sun's rays concentrated by a burning glass.   The result was exactly what he expected.   The minium turned into lead, and as an indication that it had

absorbed the phlogiston the water level in the gas jar rose dramatically.
Here surely was a demonstration that the theory corresponded with
reality.

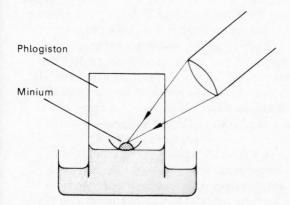

FIGURE 2   The absorption of phlogiston by lead calx

An empiricist would rightly point out that we can see the water
level rise but we do not actually see the phlogiston absorbed into the
minium.   There is no experience of seeing the gas rush into tiny pores
or crevices in its surface, as we might see bath water rush down a plug-
hole.   So the reality that the theory postulates is not visibly in accord
with the theory.   We do not have access to this area of the physical
world so we cannot see the correspondence with the theory.

The indicator of truth that we actually use is that the theory works.
We are satisfied if we achieve a smoothly operating theoretical view of
the world.   The indicator of error is the failure to establish and
maintain this working relationship of successful prediction.   One way
of putting this point would be to say that there is one sort of correspondence that we do indeed use.   This is not the correspondence of the
theory with reality but the correspondence of the theory with itself.
Experience as interpreted by the theory is monitored for such internal
consistency as is felt important.   The process of judging a theory is an
internal one.   It is not internal in the sense of being detached from
reality, for obviously the theory is connected to it by the way we
designate objects, and label and identify substances and events.   But
once the connections have been established the whole system has to
maintain a degree of coherence; one part must conform to another.

The experiment described above in fact threw up problems as well
as support for the phlogiston theory.   Priestley eventually noticed that
some drops of water had formed inside the gas jar during the experiment.
Since he had done the experiment over water these may have passed unnoticed at first.   They had certainly not been expected and their presence

indicated trouble for the theory.   Nothing in the theory had said that water would be formed, but repeating the experiment over mercury made it quite clear that it was.   Now a lack of correspondence had emerged.

No glimpse behind the scenes was needed to evoke this awareness of non-correspondence.   Reality had not deemed the theory false because of a lack of correspondence with its inner workings.   What had happened was that an anomolous situation had emerged within a given theoretical conception of the experiment.   What Priestley did was to remove the anomoly by elaborating the theory.   Once again, it was not reality that was his guide here but the theory itself, it was an internal process.   He reasoned that the minium must have contained some water that nobody had realised was there.   When it was heated this water emerged and appeared on the sides of the gas jar.   He had made a discovery about the role of water, and correspondence was now re-established.

It is interesting to compare Priestley's analysis of this experiment with our version, because as far as we are concerned his theory, and even more so its adjusted version, does not correspond with reality at all.   We do not say that the phlogiston was absorbed into the minium or that the water emerged from the minium.   We say that the gas in the jar is hydrogen and that the minium is lead oxide.   On heating, the oxygen comes out of the oxide leaving the lead.   This oxygen then combines with the hydrogen to form water.   During this formation the gas is used up and so the level of either mercury or water in the gas jar rises.

We see exactly what Priestley saw but conceive it theoretically in a quite different way.   We, no more than Priestley, have been permitted access to the hidden aspects of reality, so our view is just as much a theory.   Doubtless we are fully justified in preferring our theory because its internal coherence can be maintained over a wider range of theoretically interpreted experiments and experiences.

It is now possible to see why the relation of correspondence between a theory and reality is vague.   At no stage is this correspondence ever perceived, known or, consequently, put to any use.   We never have the independent access to reality that would be necessary if it were to be matched up against our theories.   All that we have, and all that we need, are our theories and our experience of the world;   our experimental results and our sensory-motor interactions with manipulatable objects.   No wonder that the terminology which refers to this inscrutable relation is vague, but a supposed link which plays no real part in our thinking can afford to be left vague for nothing is lost.

The processes of scientific thought can all proceed, and have to proceed. on the basis of internal principles of assessment.   They are moved by the perception of error as it crops up within the terms of our theories, purposes, interests, problems and standards.   Had Priestley not been concerned to develop a detailed account of all the events that he could detect in a chemical reaction he would have thought no more about a few drops of water if he noticed them. Similarly had we not been intent on getting more and more general theories we could have stayed content with Priestley's version. It corresponds to reality well enough for some purposes. This correspondence is only disturbed if it runs up against our requirements. The motor of change is internal to these requirements, and our theories and experience. There are as many forms of correspondence as there are requirements.

This poses a problem about the notion of truth, for why not abandon it altogether? It should be possible to see theories entirely as conventional instruments for coping with and adapting to our environment. Given that they are subject to our varying requirements of accuracy and utility, their use and development would appear to be fully explicable. What function does truth, or talk of truth, play in all this? It is difficult to see that much would be lost by its absence. There is no doubt however that it is a terminology which comes naturally and is felt to be peculiarly apt.

Our idea of truth does a number of jobs which are worth noting if only to show that they are compatible with the strong programme and the pragmatic and instrumental idea of correspondence which has emerged in the discussion. First, there is what may be called the discriminatory function. Men are under the necessity to order and sort their beliefs. They must distinguish those which work for them from those which do not. 'True' and 'false' are the labels typically used and are as good as any, although an explicitly pragmatic vocabulary would function just as well.

Second there is the rhetorical function. These labels play a role in argument, criticism and persuasion. If our knowledge were purely under the control of stimulation from the physical world there would be no problem about what to believe. But we do not mechanically adapt to the world because of the social component in our knowledge. This conventional and theoretical apparatus presents a continuing problem of maintenance. The language of truth is intimately connected with the problem of cognitive order. On the one hand, men talk of truth in general so that they may recommend this or that particular claim. On the other hand, truth is invoked precisely as an idea of something potentially different from any received opinion. It is thought of as something that transcends mere belief. It has this form because it is our way of putting a question mark against whatever we wish to doubt or change or consolidate. Of course, when men affirm truth or detect and denounce error, there is no need for them to have privileged access or ultimate insight into these things. The language of truth has never needed this. It was as available, and as legimately available to Priestley with his phlogiston theory, as it is to us.

This is all very similar to the discriminatory function except that now the labels can be seen taking on overtones of transcendence and authority. The nature of the authority can be identified immediately. In as far as any particular theoretical view of the world has authority this can only

derive from the actions and opinions of men. This is precisely where
Durkheim located the obligatory charecter of truth when he criticised
the pragmatist philosophers (see the selections in Wolff(1960) and
Giddens (1972)). Authority is a social category and only men can exert
it. They endeavour to transmit it to their settled opinions and
assumptions. Nature has power over us, but only men have authority.
In some measure the transcendence associated with truth will have the
same social source, but it also points to the third function of the notion
of truth.

    This is what may be called the materialist function. All our
thinking instinctively assumes that we exist within a common external
environment that has a determinate structure. The precise degree of
its stability is not known, but it is stable enough for many practical
purposes. The details of its working are obscure, but despite this,
much about it is taken for granted. Opinions vary about its responsive-
ness to our thoughts and actions, but in practice the existence of an
external world-order is never doubted. It is assumed to be the cause
of our experience, and the common reference of our discourse. I
shall lump all this under the name of 'materialism'. Often when we
use the word 'truth' we mean just this: how the world stands. By this
word we convey and affirm this ultimate schema with which we think.
Of course this schema is filled out in many different ways. The world
may be peopled with invisible spirits in one culture and hard, indivisible (but equally invisible) atomic particles in another. The label
of materialism is appropriate in as far as it emphasises the common
core of people, objects and natural processes which play such a
prominent role in our life. These common and prominent examples
of an external nature provide the models and exemplars by which we
give sense to more esoteric cultural theories. They provide our most
enduring, public and vivid experience of externality.

    This third function of the notion of truth can be used to overcome
an objection that may be pressed against my analysis. I have said
that men choose or question or affirm and that they count as true whatever is the outcome of these processes. This may appear to be
arguing in a circle for can these processes be described without pre-
supposing the notion of truth? Don't men question in the name of
truth, and affirm what they think is true? Surely it is wrong to use the
notion of affirming to explain the notion of truth; rather the idea of truth
is needed to make sense of affirmation. The answer is that what is
needed to make sense of affirmation is the instinctive but purely abstract
idea that the world stands somehow or other, that there are states of
affairs which can be talked about. This is what is provided by the
schema of ideas that I have called the materialist presupposition of our
thinking. All matters of substance, all issues of particular content,
have to be fought out in their own terms and independently. Whoever
wins these struggles for power helps himself to the victor's crown. In
practice, therefore, the choices and affirmations do have priority.

(The general idea of truth should never be confused with the standards that are used in any particular context to judge whether a particular claim is to be accepted as true.   This would be to assume that the mere notion of truth can act as a substantial criterion of truth. This mistake is central to Lukes's (1974) anti-relativist claims.)

That men should sort and select beliefs, that they should affirm them and garland concensus with authority, and that they should instinct- ively relate beliefs to an external environment of causes is all very easy to accept.   And it is all in conformity to the strong programme. In particular the assumption of a material world with which men establish a variety of different adaptations is exactly the picture presupposed by the pragmatic and instrumentalist notion of correspondence.   The points that have emerged can now be related, quickly, to the problem posed by Liebig and Thomson.

When we invoke truth and falsity to explain the differential success of Liebig and Thomson we are using these terms to label the different circumstances in which these men found themselves.   Liebig could generate repeatable results.   He had hit upon a way of eliciting a regular response from nature.   Thomson had not.   If one man can grow apples with no grubs in them and another cannot then, of course this may explain their differing economic fortunes - given a certain backdrop of market preferences.   Using the language of truth and falsity in order to mark such a distinction in the case of scientific work is customary and acceptable.   It is an amalgam of the functions that have just been spelled out.   It highlights causally relevent circumstances and their relation to cultural preferences and purposes.   It would be a disaster for the strong programme if it were at odds with this usage of the language of truth and falsity.   But it is not.   The use to which it is opposed is quite different viz. making an evaluation of truth and falsity and then, contingent upon that evaluation, adopting different styles of explanation for true and false beliefs.   For example, using causal explanations for error but not for truth.   This is a very different matter.   It assimilates the notion of truth to a teleological framework rather than leaving it within the causal idiom of our everyday thinking.

The idea that scientific theories, methods and acceptable results are social conventions is opposed by a number of typical arguments which must now be examined.   It is often assumed that if something is a convention then it is 'arbitrary'.   To see scientific theories and results as conventions is said to imply that they become true simply by decision and that any decision could be made.   The reply is that conventions are not arbitrary.   Not anything can be made a convention, and arbitrary decisions play little role in social life.   The constraints on what may become a convention, or a norm, or an institution, are social credibility and practical utility.   Theories must work to the degree of accuracy and within the scope conventionally expected of them.   These conventions are neither self-evident, universal or static.   Further, scientific theories and procedures must be consonant with other

conventions and purposes prevalent in a social group.   They face a
'political' problem of acceptance like any other policy recommendation.

The question may be pressed: does the acceptance of a theory by
a social group make it true?   The only answer that can be given is that
it does not.   There is nothing in the concept of truth that allows for
belief making an idea true.   Its relation to the basic materialist
picture of an independent world precludes this.   This schema
permanently holds open the gap between the knower and the known.
But if the question is rephrased and becomes: does the acceptance of a
theory make it the knowledge of a group, or does it make it the basis for
their understanding and their adaptation to the world? - the answer can
only be positive.

Another objection to seeing knowledge resting on any form of
social consensus derives from the fear that critical thought is endangered.
It has been said that on such views radical criticism is impossible
(Lukes (1974)).   What the theory in fact predicts is that the radical
criticism of the knowledge of a social group will only be possible in
certain situations.   These are, first, that more than one set of
standards and conventions are available, and more than one definition
of reality can be conceived; the second is that some motives exist for
exploiting these alternatives.   In a highly differentiated society the
first condition will always be satisfied.   In science however the second
condition will not always be satisfied.   Sometimes scientists will
calculate that more is to be gained by conformity to normal procedures
and theories than by deviance.   The factors which enter into that
calculation constitute a sociological and psychological problem in their
own right.

A simple example will serve to convey the general point that
conventions do not stand in the way of radical criticism.   Indeed without
them such criticism would be impossible.   Francis Bacon was one of
the great propagandists of science.   He along with others was a bitter
critic of what he saw as the degenerate scholasticism of the universities.
In its place he wanted to see the form of knowledge associated with the
craftsman and artisan which was useful, practical and active.   He thus
used the standards, habits and interests and conventions of one section
of society as the yardstick with which to measure other types of learning.
He did not search for, nor would he have found, any supra-social
standards.   There is no Archimedian point.

If the condition of reflexivity is to be satisfied it ought to be
possible to apply this whole account to the sociology of knowledge itself
without in any way undermining it.   This certainly is possible.   There
is no reason why a sociologist or any other scientist should be ashamed
to see his theories and methods as emanating from society, that is, as
the product of collective influences and resources and as peculiar to his
culture and its present circumstances.   Indeed if a sociologist tried to
evade this realisation he would be denigrating the subject-matter of his
own science.   There is certainly nothing about such an admission that

entails that science should be unresponsive to experience or careless of facts. After all, what are the conventional requirements currently imposed by the social milieu on any science? They are what we take for granted as the scientific method as it is practised in the various disciplines.

To say that the methods and results of science are conventions does not make them 'mere' conventions. This would be to commit the unspeakable blunder of thinking that conventions are things that are trivially satisfied and essentially undemanding. Nothing could be more mistaken. Conventional demands frequently stretch men to the very limit of their physical and mental capacities. An extreme case will serve as a reminder: think of the feats of endurance that North American Indian males were said to undergo in order to be fully initiated warriors of their tribe. That theories and scientific ideas be properly adapted to the conventional requirements that are expected of them means, among other things, that they make successful predictions. This is a harsh discipline to impose on our mental constitution; but it is no less a convention.

Doubtless the feeling will linger that some form of lewdness has been committed. It will still be said that truth has been reduced to mere social convention. This feeling is the motive force behind all the detailed arguments against the sociology of knowledge that have been examined in the last two chapters. These arguments have been faced and rejected, but perhaps the feeling remains. Let us therefore take it as a phenomenon in its own right and try to explain its presence. Its very existence may reveal something interesting about science - for something in the nature of science must provoke this protective and defensive response.

Chapter 3

SOURCES OF RESISTANCE TO
THE STRONG PROGRAMME

Suppose that some of the detailed objections to the sociology of
scientific knowledge had proved insurmountable, what would this have
meant?   It would have meant that there was a most striking oddity and
irony at the very heart of our culture.   If sociology could not be applied
in a thorough-going way to scientific knowledge it would mean that
science could not scientifically know itself.   Whilst the knowledge of
other cultures, and the non-scientific elements of our own culture can
be known via science, science itself, of all things, cannot be afforded
the same treatment.   This would make it a special case, a standing
exception to the generality of its own procedures.

Those who taunt the sociology of knowledge with self-refutation
can only propose their arguments because they are prepared to accept
a self-imposed limitation on science itself.   Why should anyone be
prepared to do this?   How is it that it can feel right and proper to make
science an exception to itself when unrestricted generality would seem
to be so obviously desirable?   When these questions have been investigated I believe that the source of all the detailed arguments against the
strong programme will have been located.

In order to understand the forces producing this strange feature
in our cultural attitudes it will be necessary to develop a theory about
the origin and nature of our feelings about science.   To do this I shall
appeal to Durkheim's 'The Elementary Forms of the Religious Life'
(1915).   The theory that I shall advance will depend on an analogy
between science and religion.

A DURKHEIMEAN APPROACH TO SCIENCE

The reason for resisting the scientific investigation of science can be
illuminated by appeal to the distinction between the sacred and the
profane.   For Durkheim the distinction is at the very heart of religious
phenomena.   He says:

But the real characteristic of religious phenomena is that
they always suppose a bipartite division of the whole universe,
known and knowable, into two classes which embrace all
that exists, but which radically exclude each other. Sacred
things are those which the interdictions protect and isolate;
profane things, those to which these interdictions are applied
and which must remain at a distance from the first. Religious
beliefs are the representations which express the nature of
sacred things and the relations which they sustain, either
with each other or with profane things (p. 56).

The puzzling attitude towards science would be explicable if it were
being treated as sacred, and as such, something to be kept at a respect-
ful distance. This is perhaps why its attributes are held to transcend
and defy comparison with all that is not science but merely belief,
prejudice, habit, error or confusion. The workings of science are
then assumed to proceed from principles neither grounded in, nor comparable with, those operating in the profane world of politics and power.

Is it not strange to use a religious metaphor to illuminate science?
Are they not antagonistic principles? The metaphor may seem both
inappropriate and offensive. Those who find in science the very
epitome of knowledge are unlikely to grant religion equal validity and
so may be expected to view the comparison with distaste. This
reaction would miss the point which is to make a comparison between
two spheres of social life, and to suggest that similar principles are
at work in both. The aim is not to diminish one or the other, or to
embarrass the practitioners of either field. Religious behaviour is
built around the distinction between the sacred and the profane and the
manifestations of this distinction are similar to the stance frequently
taken towards science. This point of contact means that other insights
about religion may also be applicable.

If science is indeed treated as if it is sacred does this explain why
it should not be applied to itself? Cannot the sacred come into contact
with itself? Where is the process of profanation which requires the
sociologist to avert his gaze from science? One way in which this
question may appear to be answered is as follows. Many philosophers
and scientists do not count the sociology of knowledge as part of science
at all. Hence it belongs to the sphere of the profane and to bring it to
bear on science proper would be to bring the profane into contact with
the sacred. But this reply begs the crucial question - why in the first
place is the sociology of knowledge considered to be outside of science?
The argument of the previous chapters has been that nothing about the
methods of sociology should exclude it from science. This suggests
that its subject-matter is responsible for its exclusion. Perhaps,
then, the tendency to deny it the priviliged status of science is not
fortuitous. The sociology of knowledge does not merely happen to be
outside of science, and hence pose a threat. Rather, it has to be outside of science because its chosen subject-matter makes it threatening:

it threatens by its very nature. Similarly it may be suggested that the
sociology of knowledge is not counted as a science because it is very
young and underdeveloped. This lack of stature excludes it from science,
and hence it is profane and causes a threat. This again begs a crucial
question, for why is it so underdeveloped? Is it not perhaps retarded
because there is a positive disinclination to examine the nature of
knowledge in a candid and scientific way? In other words the sociology
of knowledge does not pose a threat because it is underdeveloped, it is
underdeveloped because it poses a threat.

These considerations lead back to the original issue: why should
the sacred character of scientific knowledge be threatened by a
sociological scrutiny? The answer lies in a further articulation of the
idea of the sacred.

Religion is essentially a source of strength. When men
communicate with their gods they are fortified, elevated and protected.
Strength flows from religious objects and rites - strength not merely to
engage in more sacred practices but to continue with day-to-day profane
ones. Furthermore, man is a creature conceived by religion as
consisting of two parts, a soul and a body. The soul is that within him
which partakes of the sacred and it is different in nature to the rest of
his mind and body. This remainder, which is profane, has to be
severely controlled and ritually prepared before it comes into the
vicinity of the sacred.

This essential religious duality of man is similar to a duality which
is often attributed to knowledge. Science is not all of a piece. It is
subject to a duality of nature which is signalised by many distinctions,
e.g. that between pure and applied, science and technology, theory and
practice, popular and serious, routine and fundamental. In general we
may say that knowledge has its sacred aspects and its profane side, like
human nature itself. Its sacred aspects represent whatever we deem to
be highest in it. These may be its central principles and methods; or
they may be its greatest achievements or its purest ideational contents
stated in abstraction from all detail concerning origin or evidence or
past confusions. As an illustration notice how the great physiologist
du Bois-Reymond uses the idea of the boundary or threshold between pure
and applied work and how he invokes the spirituality of learning. In a
lecture published in 1912 he argued that a training in pure research has
a value 'which accrues even to the mediocre mind, that, at least once in
his life before the overwhelming attraction of practical studies seizes
him, he has been compelled to one step over the threshold of pure learning and has felt the breath of its spirit; that at least once he has seen the
truth sought, found, and cherished for its own sake' (quoted in Turner
(1971)).

Just as strength derived from contact with the sacred must be
carried forth into the world so the sacred aspects of science can be
thought of as informing or guiding the more mundane, less inspired,
less vital parts. These latter are its routines, its mere applications,

its settled external forms of technique and method.   But, of course, the source of religious strength to operate in the profane world must never give the believer such a degree of confidence that he forgets the crucial distinction between the two.   He must never forget his ultimate dependence on the sacred.   He must never believe that he is self-sufficient and that his .power will not require regenerating.   By analogy the routines of science must not ever assume self-sufficiency which overlooks their need to derive strength from a source of a different and more powerful nature.   On this view the practice of science must not become so important in its own estimate that it reduces everything to the same level.   There must always be a source of strength from which energy flows outwards and with which contact can and must be renewed.

The threat posed by the sociology of knowledge is precisely this: it appears to reverse or interfere with the outward flow of energy and inspiration which derives from contact with the basic truths and principles of science and methodology.   What derives from these principles, namely the practice of science, is essentially less sacred and more profane than the source itself.   Hence to turn an activity in-formed by these principles on to the principles themselves is profanation and contamination.   Only ruin can ensue.

This is the answer to the puzzle that science is most enthusiastic-ally advocated by precisely those who welcome least its application to itself.   Science is sacred, so it must be kept apart.   It is, as I shall sometimes say 'reified' or 'mystified'.   This protects it from pollution which would destroy its efficacy, authority and strength as a source of knowledge.

So far I have only offered an explanation that would apply to scientific enthusiasts.   What about the humanistic and literary traditions in our culture?   Thinkers in this tradition are perfectly willing to grant science its place in our system of knowledge, but their conception of that place is different from that of the enthusiasts.   The humanists are sensitive to the limitations of science and to any implausible pretentions that may be entertained on its behalf.   The claims of other forms of knowledge are vigorously pressed.   For example: our everyday knowledge of people and things.   This, it is said, has a stability which far exceeds scientific theorising and is marvellously adapted to the subtleties of the material and social world as we daily encounter them.   Philosophers of common sense and humanism are often in complete agreement with philosophers of science in their criticisms of the sociology of knowledge. An explanation in terms of the sacredness of science clearly cannot apply to the humanists, but their position can still be analysed in similar Durkheimean terms.   What is sacred for them is something non-scientific, such as the common sense or the given form of a culture. Hence if science tries to concern itself with these topics, then it is resisted by philosophical argument.   This response will be provoked from the humanistic philosopher, whether the encroaching science be physics, physiology, economics or sociology.   The forms of knowledge which are hedged around by these thinkers are typically the art of the poet, novelist, playwright, painter or musician.   These, it is held, convey the really significant truths which it is man's business in life to learn and by which he can sustain himself.   (Exponents of 'linguistic analysis' in philosophy furnish many examples of this humanistic approach. Thus Ryle's 'Concept of Mind' (1949) can be read as a defence of the priority and permanence of the psychological insights of novelists like Jane Austen.)

SOCIETY AND KNOWLEDGE

The hypothesis has been advanced that science and knowledge are typically afforded the same treatment as believers give to the sacred. So far the only justification for this hypothesis has been that, if it is granted, then a puzzling feature of our intellectual values can be rendered comprehensible.   This is not a negligible gain in its own right, and perhaps the oddity of the fact it seeks to explain is sufficient justification for the apparent oddity of the hypothesis itself.   But even that sense of oddity may be diminished by pressing the analysis still further.

The question must be asked: why should knowledge ever be accorded such an exalted status as has been assumed in the above hypothesis? Here it is necessary to develop a fuller picture of the role of knowledge in society and our available resources for thinking about it and forming attitudes towards it.   I shall use Durkheim's general thesis about the origin and nature of religious experience viz. that religion is essentially a way of perceiving, and making intelligible our experience of, the society in which we live.   Durkheim suggests that: 'Before all, (religion) is a system of ideas with which the individuals represent to themselves the society of which they are members, and the obscure but intimate relations which they have with it' (p. 257).   The distinction between the sacred and the profane marks off those objects and practices which symbolise the principles on which the society is organised.   They embody the power of its collective force - a force which can energise and sustain its members, or which can impinge on them as a constraint of peculiar and awesome efficacy.   Thus:

> Since it is in spiritual ways that social pressure exercises itself, it could not fail to give men the idea that outside themselves there exist one or several powers, both moral and, at the same time, efficacious, upon which they depend.   They must think of these powers, at least in part, as outside themselves, for these address them in a tone of command and sometimes even order them to do violence to their most natural inclinations.   It is undoubtedly true that if they were able to see that these influences which they feel emanate from society, then the mythological system of interpretations would never be born.   But social action follows ways that are too circuitous and obscure, and employs psychical mechanisms

that are too complex to allow the ordinary observer to see whence it comes. As long as scientific analysis does not come to teach it to them, men know well that they are acted upon, but they do not know by whom. So they must invent by themselves the idea of those powers with which they feel themselves in connection, and from that, we are able to catch a glimpse of the way by which they were led to represent them under forms that are really foreign to their nature and to transfigure them by thought (p. 239).

Durkheim's powerful vision can be put to work by supposing that when men think about the nature of knowledge, what they are doing is indirectly reflecting on the principles according to which society is organised. Indeed, they are tacitly manipulating images of society. In their minds, structuring and guiding their thoughts, are conceptions whose real character is that of a social model. Just as religious experience transmutes our experience of society, so on my hypothesis does philosophy, epistemology or any general conceptions of knowledge. So the answer to the question of why knowledge should ever be seen as sacred is that in thinking about knowledge we are thinking about society, and if Durkheim is right, society tends to be perceived as sacred.

In order to see if accounts of knowledge really do appear to have the character of transfigured conceptions of society it will obviously be necessary to look at particular cases. This will be done in the next chapter, but a number of points need to be discussed by way of preparation.

First, to say that we think about knowledge by manipulating images of society does not mean that it is a conscious process or that it will necessarily be apparent in every epistemological or philosophical investigation. The direction of a line cannot be guessed from a small segment, and basic social models may not emerge in detailed or isolated arguments. The social models will only be clear in work of a broad scope.

Second, what is the initial plausibility of the connection that I have postulated? Why should social models be used when thinking about knowledge? These questions can be partly answered by stressing the need for some model and partly by suggesting that social models are especially appropriate - that there is a natural affinity between the two groups of ideas.

To think about the nature of knowledge is at once to immerse oneself in an abstract and obscure enterprise. To ask questions of the sort which philosophers address to themselves is usually to paralyse the mind. Thinking in this sphere badly needs something to appeal to that is familiar and which can provide a framework on which thoughts may hang. Even if the nature of scientific knowledge is treated in a very concrete way as it is by historians, still a similar problem occurs. Organising principles are necessary if the data is to be marshalled into a coherent story. History presupposes a picture of science just as much as it gives one and it is to some tacit philosophy or to the tradition of various schools of philosophy, that the historian typically turns.

Even if it is granted that a model of some sort is necessary why should a picture of society be an appropriate pattern for an account of knowledge? Why should the mind lean on what it knows about society when it is perplexed by the nature of knowledge? Part of the answer lies in the circumstances under which we become perplexed about knowledge in the first place. These are typically when rival claims to provide knowledge are offered by different social groups such as the church and the laity, the academic and the layman, the specialist and the generalist, the powerful and the weak, the established and the dissenting. Furthermore there are many intuitive connections between knowledge and society. Knowledge has to be gathered, organised, sustained, transmitted and distributed. These are all processes visibly connected with established institutions: the laboratory, the workplace, the university, the church, the school. The mind will thus have registered on some level a connection between knowledge and authority and power. Rigid authority and control in the sphere of knowledge seems more likely when those same charecteristics are present in society at large than does, say, fluidity, easy choice and liberal alternatives of belief. A sense of analogy and proportion connects our ideas of knowledge and society. Indeed, in our unreflective minds, these may not be separate things at all.

That extravagant philosopher-patriot Fichte provides an illustration of how knowledge is swept up in social and theological categories. The University, he said, in a rectorial address at Berlin in 1811, 'is the visible representation of the immortality of our race'; it is 'the most holy thing that the human race possesses'. Like the previous, and more muted, illustration from du Bois-Reymond this is also from Turner's study of the growth of professorial research in Prussia. It may well be that these sentiments, or their intensity, are conditioned by the time and place of their utterance. But in my argument they are meant as reminders: we are not, perhaps, as unused to emitting or decoding messages of this kind as we may think.

Here an objection may be raised. If knowledge is too abstract a thing to reflect about directly - hence the need for social models - then why isn't society too overwhelming a thing to think about directly? Why don't we need a model for society too? This question suggests a valuable addition that can be made to the account which is emerging - for surely the suggestion is true. Immersed as we are in society we cannot grasp it as a whole in our reflective consciousness except by using a simplified picture, an image, or what may be called an 'ideology'. Religion in Durkheim's sense represents an ideology of this sort. This means that the dimly perceived sense of identity between knowledge and society in fact provides a channel through which our simplified social ideologies make contact with our theories of knowledge. It is these ideologies rather than the totality of our real social experience which might be expected to control and structure our theories of knowledge.

What has just been outlined is a theory about how people think. The hypotheses are not alleged to be necessary truths. Their substantial character means that they cannot be proved to be true but only more or less supported by inductive evidence. Furthermore the range of application of the picture here presented, has yet to be determined. The tendency to reify or mystify depends on conditions which are not fully known, though it will be necessary as the argument proceeds to venture another hypothesis to deal with this topic.

In order to provide support for the position developed in this chapter I shall analyse two important modern theories about the nature of knowledge and show how they depend on social images and metaphors. This will be the aim of the next chapter. At the end of the chapter I shall discuss the conditions under which it should be possible to overcome the feeling that scientific knowledge is too objective to be investigated sociologically.

Chapter 4

KNOWLEDGE AND SOCIAL IMAGERY: A CASE STUDY

In this chapter I shall examine a long-standing debate between two rival conceptions of science. My purpose is to bring out the way in which social images and metaphors govern these rival claims, determining their style, content and relations to one another. One position is that of Sir Karl Popper, as stated in his classic book 'The Logic of Scientific Discovery' (1959) and elaborated in later work. The other position is that developed by T.S. Kuhn in his controversial 'The Structure of Scientific Revolution' (1962). My concern here will be with the overall structure of their positions rather than with matters of detail (but for details see Lakatos and Musgrave (1970)).

Since the debate has been going on for some ten years, and has long reached stalemate I shall not attempt to contribute to the debate itself. At this stage such an approach is not likely to meet with much success (and I have had my say in Bloor (1971)). Instead I shall concentrate on putting the debate into a much wider perspective than usual by relating it to long-standing controversies in economics, jurisprudence, political theory and ethics. I believe that the character of the epistemological debate cannot fully be understood without seeing it as an expression of deep ideological concerns in our culture.

THE POPPER-KUHN DEBATE

Sir Karl Popper's conception of science is clear and cogent. The aim of science is to grasp significant truths about the world, and to do this we must formulate powerful theories. These are conjectures about the nature of reality which solve problems created by the violation of our expectations. Some expectations may be inborn but most of them derive from previously held theories. Thus if science starts with tacit assumptions these will soon become conscious. As part of the conscious process of theory construction we are at liberty to use any material we wish: myth, prejudice or guess. What matters is what we do with our theories not where they come from.

Once a theory has been formulated it must be severely criticised
by logical scrutiny and empirical test. Logical criticism cuts down
obscurity and draws forth the claims that are contained in a theory.
Empirical testing requires that the general statements of theories be
combined with statements describing the test situation. Provided that
the theory is sufficiently precise it should now be possible to seek out
weakness in the theory by trying to falsify its predictions. If it passes
the test it is corroborated and can be retained for the time being.

The importance of testing theories resides in the fact that
knowledge does not come easily to us. We have to strive in order to
know, for without effort we should be left with superficial and erroneous
speculations. But the effort we expend on our theories must be critical
effort. To protect our theories against the world would be dogmatism
and would lead to an illusory sense of knowledge. As far as science is
concerned, the objects and processes of the world have no fixed essence
which can be grasped once and for all. Thus science is not only a
critical struggle, it is an unending one. Science would lose its
empirical character and become metaphysics if it ceased to change.
Truth is indeed the goal, but it is at an infinite distance.

The tone and style of Popper's philosophy is an important part of
its overall message. This tone is in part provided by the key
metaphors which are used. The image of Darwinian struggle is
prominent. Science is a projection of this struggle for survival, but
one in which our theories die for us. To speed up the struggle for
survival and the elimination of weak theories we are enjoined to take
intellectual risks. On the negative side various sources of authority
are criticised. Science does not subordinate itself to the authority of
either reason or experience. Both are unreliable guides to the truth.
What appears self-evident to the reason of one generation will be
contingent or even false to the next. Our experiences may be quite mis-
leading and the meaning attributed to an experimental result may change
radically. Another aspect of the anti-authoritarian side of Popper's
work is the image of the unity of mankind - in this case the 'rational
unity of mankind'. No individual or type speaks with more authority
than any other. Nobody is a privileged source of truth; all claims must
be subject alike to criticism and test.

The style of Popper's thought resides in the insistence that
progress can be made, problems solved, issues clarified and decided
given sufficient critical effort. Popper's own work is an example, for
he has brought to light the rules of the scientific game and delineated the
errors which might lead to dogmatism and obscurantism. As part of
this process of codification Popper lays down certain important criteria
and boundaries. Most important is the criterion of testability or
falsifiability. This separates scientific assertions from pseudo-
scientific or metaphysical claims. Metaphysics is not meaningless but
it is unscientific. It belongs, so to speak, to the private sphere of
individual preference. Psychologically it may be an important source
of inspiration but it must not be confused with science itself.

Other boundaries and barriers such as those between specialities are treated quite differently. The blight of specialisation represents an artificial barrier to the free traffic of ideas. Bold theories may well cross these barriers and ought not to be impeded. Again, the barriers imposed by different theoretical idioms or languages is one for which Popper reserves contempt. Anything of substance can be translated from one theoretical language to another. Languages do not contain mysterious resources for capturing truths which are unstatable in other terms. The rational unity of mankind has no respect for theoretical language or idiom.

This rigorous conception of science has, and surely deserves, a wide appeal. It clearly captures many of the values which anyone with a commitment to science would naturally want to endorse.

Professor Kuhn's conception of science shares with Popper's the quality of having a simple and compelling overall structure within which issues of detail are worked out with great sophistication. The main focus of his analysis concerns what he calls a 'paradigm'. A paradigm is an exemplary piece of scientific work which creates a research tradition within some specialised area of scientific activity. The paradigm investigation provides a working model of how to do science in some area, giving concrete guidance on experimental method, apparatus and theoretical interpretation. Variations and elaborations will be developed to wring further results out of nature. This process of growth around the paradigm will clearly not be one of mechanical duplication. The subtle relations between the different experiments modelled around a paradigmatic contribution will be easier to see than to state. Their connections will form a network of analogies and 'family resemblances'.

The tradition which grows around a paradigm will constitute, for some limited but indeterminate area of research, a relatively autonomous set of activities which Kuhn calls 'normal science'. Normal science is predicated on the success and worth of the paradigm and in no way seeks to call it into question. It corresponds to a state of mind which sees the furtherance of the research tradition as giving rise to puzzles rather than problems. To call something a puzzle assumes that a solution exists and in this case it carries the further implication that the terms of the solution will be similar to those that have already proved successful in the paradigm investigations itself. But the puzzles of normal science cannot be achieved by the application of any set of 'rules'. Nor are the solutions implicitly contained in or entailed by the paradigm investigation. Normal science is essentially creative, for it has to manufacture for itself as it goes along the required extensions to the original investigation on which it is modelled. Kuhn likens this creative but constrained activity to the application of a legal precedent in case-law.

Kuhn sees normal science as a succession of successful puzzle solutions. It is this cumulative success which gives the researcher the confidence and background of experience to press his experiments even further into the esoteric details of his subject matter.   It is the growth of the theoretical aspects of the research tradition which give these details their meaning and permits them to cohere in a significant way.

Such confidence and commitment born of past success will not be shaken by the occasional failure to bring an anomaly within the scope of what may, by now, be a greatly elaborated paradigm.   Failure to solve a puzzle reflects, in the first instance, on the competence of the individual researcher.   An unresolved anomaly may come to be seen as a particularly complicated case that can be legitimately left aside for the time being.   If, however, the perspective of the paradigm offers no reason why the unresolved anomaly should cause so much trouble, and should the problem appear ripe for solution and yet still resist the efforts of the most accomplished practitioners, then a crisis of confidence may ensue.   The anomaly will become a special focus of concern, the empirical aspects of the untamed phenomenon will be examined with redoubled effort, and increasingly eccentric theorising will be necessary in order to grasp its significance.   The pattern of growth of normal science will have been disrupted and a different atmosphere will prevail - an atmosphere which Kuhn calls 'extra-ordinary science'.

In order to resolve the crisis a new model for doing science in the troubled area may be generated.   The community of specialists may come to accept a new paradigm for research provided it accommodates the crucial anomaly.   If this happens then Kuhn speaks of a 'revolution'. A revolution in science occurs when a community of specialists decide that the new paradigm holds out a better promise for future development than does the old one.   What is involved in making such a decision?   It is necessary to have a deep intellectual grasp of the details of the field in order to assess the depth of the crisis in the old procedures and the promise of the new.   But the intellectual aspects of the decision have to be accompanied by a judgment.   The relative weights to be attached to the various reasons for or against a change of scientific strategy can only be justified to a certain degree.   Justification has to stop some-where and a step made which has no justification, for proof is not to be had.   Nor can the scientist depend on much help from outside his speciality because the community itself is the locus of relevant knowledge and experience.   It is the last court of appeal.

As with Popper's work, Kuhn's account of science has a definite flavour which is at least partly caused by the metaphors which the author finds it natural to use.   Scientists form a 'community' of practitioners.   The theme of 'community' is a pervasive one, with its overtones of social solidarity, of a settled way of life with its own style, habits and routines.   This theme is only reinforced by its contrast to the controversial imagery of the 'revolution' which periodically over-takes the community.   There is in Kuhn no campaign against the notion of authority, indeed in one of his formulations the useful function of dogma in science is remarked on.   The process of scientific education is presented as authoritarian.   It does not seek to present the student with an impartial account of rival views of the world associated with previous paradigms.   Rather it seeks to make him capable of working within the existing paradigm.

Kuhn's approach does not suggest that everything about science can be made explicit and clear.   Science is a set of concrete practices rather than an activity with an explicit methodology.   In the last analysis science is a pattern of behaviour and judgment whose grounds do not lie in any abstract verbal statements of universal standards.   Those features of science which are conducted at the level of explicit verbalisation, such as its explicit theorising, utilise concepts which are deeply anchored in paradigmatic practices.   A change of paradigm will therefore be accompanied by changes in language and meaning.   The problems of translation across paradigm boundaries are deep ones and may not be totally surmountable.

Here, then, are two very different accounts of science.   The differences are undeniable and yet there is a vast area of common ground. Indeed, the amount of factual dispute about what actually goes on in science is quite small.   Popper draws attention to dramatic conjectures and severe tests, e.g. Einstein's prediction that light will bend in the vicinity of massive bodies.   Kuhn does not deny the existence or the importance of those events but stresses the background which makes them possible and gives them their significance.   Popper for his part does not deny the existence of 'normal science' but he does insist that it is hack work.   Consider also their attitude towards protracted theoretical disputes, for example over the theory of matter.   These are central to the sciences of physics and chemistry in Popper's account. For Kuhn such battles suggest a state of extraordinary science, and hence should be rare.   Where protracted disputes do seem to take place, Kuhn argues that they concern metaphysical matters rather than issues within science proper.   They have little real influence on how science is actually practised.   This, of course, accentuates Kuhn's tendency to see science as a set of concrete localised practices, whilst Popper's reading accentuates its critical character.

It would appear that a wide range of facts can be accommodated in either scheme, although their significance will be seen differently.   It is a matter of some subtlety to define the exact points of difference between the two approaches and Kuhn states the point well when he says that what divides him from Popper is a Gestalt switch: the same facts are fitted together to form a different picture.

Two important points of interpretation on which Kuhn and Popper agree concern truth and the nature of fact.   These are worth discussing briefly because they may be thought to constitute major differences between the two, when really they do not do so at all.   First, it is sometimes said that Kuhn is undermining the objectivity of science because he does not believe in the existence of pure facts (Scheffler (1967)).   There is for Kuhn no stable, independent court of appeal against which theories can be judged.   What counts as a fact is paradigm-dependent.   The meaning and significance of experiences and experimental results are consequences of our orientation to the world and it is commitment to the paradigm which provides that orientation.   However, on the level of epistemology, Popper also accepts that facts are not simple things given to us in unproblematic, direct experience of the world.   For Popper any report of an observation or an experiemental result has exactly the same logical status as the hypothesis that it may be used to test.   Theories are tested by what he calls 'observational hypothesis'.   The statements which make up the observational basis of science are indeed prompted by experience.   But for Popper this is merely a fact about the cause of our accepting an (observational) hypothesis.   Experience does not provide a reason, let alone a decisive reason for adopting an observational report.   Every statement goes beyond the experience which prompts it and hence acts as a conjectural generalisation.   This analysis is entirely in accord with the sharp boundary that Popper draws between the origin of larger-scale hypotheses and the reasons for accepting them, for the time being, as true.   Experience is an irrational cause for low-level hypothesis just as, say, religious experience may be an irrational cause for a cosmological hypothesis.   In regard to 'facts' then both Popper and Kuhn are considerably more sceptical than common sense, both believe in the 'theoretical' nature of facts.

Second, it may appear that Kuhn robs science of the role of providing us with truths, for is not science an endless progression of paradigms with no guarantee that one is truer than another?   There is, after all, no access to the world independent of science against which the progress of paradigms might be measured.   But Popper is in exactly the same position.   Truth is an ideal or goal but it is at an infinite distance. No guarantees can be provided by either account to ensure progress towards the goal of truth.   Both accounts are ways of removing perceived errors.   Both are frankly sceptical about science's grasp of anything stable and final.   The treatment of fact and truth does not differentiate the two accounts in any profound way.

Nevertheless the divergence between the two accounts is consider-able.   It can be located in the following points.   First, there is a different weight accorded to their prescriptive and descriptive aspects. Popper is undeniably laying down methodological prescriptions.   At the same time it is science whose procedures he is specifying and so there must be, and there surely is, contact with the reality of scientific practice.   Kuhn is much closer to a descriptive account with no overt legislation involved.   Yet when pressed he states clearly that his account is also an account of how science ought to be done.   So both are pre-scriptive and descriptive, but in different proportions and flavours.

Second, Popper stresses debate, disagreement and criticism whilst Kuhn stresses the taken-for-granted areas of agreement.   In other words, both attend to the social nature of science but the social processes that are uppermost in their minds are different - for one it is public debate for the other it is a shared way of life.

Third, Popper focuses on those aspects of science which are universal and abstract, such as its methodological canons and general intellectual values.   Kuhn focuses on its local and concrete aspects such as the specific pieces of work which provide exemplars for groups of practitioners.

Fourth, Popper's vision of science sees it as a linear, homogeneous process.   The same methods and processes apply to all stages. It expands in content and power, each step an addition and a progression towards its infinitely remote goal.   Kuhn, by contrast, has a cyclical conception.   Instead of a uniform bustle of activity there is a cycle of qualitatively different procedures, although the emphasis in undoubtedly on the tranquil but flexible routine of normal science.   Whilst Popper's scientists look towards the future, the Kuhnian scientist normally works by precedent.   His point of reference is in the past.

ENLIGHTENMENT VERSUS ROMANTIC IDEOLOGIES

The debate in the philosophy of science that I have just sketched is structurally identical to debates which have gone on for some two hundred years in the realms of political, social, economic, ethical and legal theory.   Indeed the clash between Popper and Kuhn represents an almost pure case of the opposition between what may be called the Enlightenment and Romantic ideologies.   (My specification of the ideologies is taken in the first instance from Mannheim's fine essay on Conservative Thought (1953).)

What I am going to call 'Enlightenment' social thought typically appeals to the notion of a 'social contract'.   This may be the alleged historical genesis of society or it may be a way of characterising the obligations and rights which fall upon members of society.   Corresponding to the myth of the social contract there is the myth of the pre-social 'state of nature'.   Sometimes this is thought of as a more - or - less brutish state from which society rescued man.   With more sophistication it is presented as the state into which man will lapse if society should break down.   Associated with the state of nature or with the social contract, there is a body of natural and inalienable rights, e.g. to life, liberty and property.   The details of these rights and the way in which the metaphor of the contract is handled vary considerably but the general theme is a typical one for eighteenth-century writers.

More important, and more enduring, than the substantial natural law doctrines is the methodological style of Enlightenment thought.   This has four characteristics.   First, it is individualistic and atomistic.   This means that it conceives of wholes and collectivities as being unproblem- atically equivalent to sets of individual units.   The nature of the units is unchanged by being brought together.   Thus societies are collections of individuals whose essential nature and individuality is not bound up with society.   For example, an individual person is made up of his reasoning or calculating faculty and a set of needs and desires, plus, of course, his kit of natural rights. These are not thought of as varying from society to society or as different in different historical epochs. Second, this individualism is closely associated with a certain static approach to thinking. Historical variation is subordinated to a concern for the timeless and the universal. Rationality and morality, man's propensity to seek pleasure and avoid pain, are unchanging and can be abstracted from the confusion of the contingent and the concrete. These points are intimately related to the third feature of Enlightenment thought, which might be called its abstract deductivism. Typically, particular social phenomena or cases of individual behaviour are illuminated by being related to abstract general principles whether of morality or reasoning or scientific law. A fourth and final manifestation of great importance, concerns the employment of the features just described. Because Enlightenment thinking is often, though not always, associated with reform, education and change it tends to have a strong prescriptive and moralising flavour. It is not meant to be the vehicle for a neutral description, but a way in which a reforming 'ought' can be made to confront the recalcitrant 'is' of society. Associated with this moral purpose is the atomising, analytical tendency which can be used to break up fixed and stable patterns of connection and association. The abstract universalism of the Enlightenment style enables it to hold up clear, general principles whose very distance from reality can serve as a reproach to the latter and a goal for action. It will emerge later that it can serve other purposes too.

What may be called 'Romantic' thinking by contrast finds no place for an apparatus of natural rights, social contracts or states of nature. The notion of pre-social naturalness is replaced by the idea of the essentially social nature of man. It is society which is natural. The calculating overtones of the social contract are replaced by the organic image of family unity. Family relationships, on this view, suggest that rights, duties, obligations and authority ought not to be spread uniformly. They should be unequally distributed according to generation, rank and role. Furthermore, justice is not created in the family by means of a constitution or by contractual bargaining. It more naturally adopts an autocratic but flexible and benevolent form, being gradually adjusted to the changing ages, responsibilities and conditions of its members.

The methodological style of Romantic thought can be contrasted point by point with that of Enlightenment thinking. First, it is not atomistic or individualistic. Social wholes are not treated as mere collections of individuals but are seen as having properties of a special kind, e.g. certain spirits, traditions, styles and national characteristics. These require and justify independent study, for the way they develop and flower might easily be missed. Those who focus too closely on the isolated atoms will fail to observe the overall patterns and their laws. Individuals can only be understood in context. Second, this sense of context leads to the belief that the concrete and the historical are more important than the universal and the timeless. The notion of the universal principles of reason is replaced by that of the locally conditioned variation of responses and adaptations, and by the belief in the historically conditioned and developing nature of all the products of creative thought.   Third, in the place of abstract deductive procedures which bring particular cases under abstract, general laws there is stress on concrete individuality.   The particular case, provided it is viewed in all its concrete individuality, is thought of as more real than abstract principles.   The fourth characteristic is the counterpart of the moralistic and normative tendency of Enlightenment thought.   The analytical, dissolving clarity of the latter is counterposed by an insistence on the reality of features of society which tend to be ignored by the more abstract stance.   The wholeness, the intricacy, the interconnection of social practices is stressed.   The frequent posture of defence and reaction adopted by Romantic thinkers serves to weld together its descriptive and prescriptive components.   Values tend to be seen as immanent, blended and united with facts.

It is easy to demonstrate that Popper must be classed as an Enlightenment thinker and Kuhn as a Romantic thinker.   Popper is individualistic and atomistic in that he treats science as a collection of isolated theories.   Little attention is paid to traditions of theory construction, to continuities within traditions or to discontinuities between different epochs in science.   His unit of analysis is the individual theoretical conjecture.   The logical and methodological characteristics of these units appear to be the same in all cases and at all stages of scientific investigation.   Further, he is concerned with the timeless and universal attributes of good scientific thinking.   Any place or time will furnish examples, whether it be pre-Socratic philosophy or modern physics.   The individual case is to be appraised by relating it to abstract canons of rationality or timeless criteria of demarcation.   The prescriptive preoccupations of Popper's thought have already been remarked upon.   Finally a parallel can be found in Popper's conception of science to the myth of the social contract.   This emerges in the details of his theory of the 'observational base' of science which has already been briefly described.   Popper characterises this base by saying that there is a 'decision' by the scientific community to 'accept' certain basic statements as facts, for the time being.   A 'decision' is involved because really these statements are hypotheses like all statements in science. The process is likened to a jury decision (1959, p. 108-9).   This is of course only an analogy and it is not offered as historical fact.   Nevertheless such a flight into analogy, especially one of this particular sort, is surely not fortuitous.   Just like the appeal to contractual 'decisions' to set up society it reveals a certain cast of mind and corresponds to a certain style and direction of analysis.   It means that at precisely the point where it would be obvious to appeal to natural processes and to ask psychological and sociological questions, the investigation is arbitrarily closed.   Too easily, 'contracts' and 'decisions' can be construed as points rather than as processes; as things without structure or history;

as momentary events. Seen in this way they can function as discontinuities which terminate enquiry.

The Romantic aspects of Kuhn's account are also very clear.
Individual scientific ideas are always part of the embracing 'whole' of
the research tradition. The community aspects of science feature
prominently and with it the authoritarian character of the educational
process. In this account there are no clear cut logical cum methodological processes of falsification. Intuitive judgment is always involved
in responding to an anomaly and deciding whether or not it constitutes a
threat to established approaches. Nor are abstract principles of
procedure to be found in theory development. This is because paradigms
are not statable theories. Research traditions do not have written
constitutions. Historical and cultural variation from speciality to
speciality is taken for granted. Finally the descriptive flavour of Kuhn's
account, where the prescriptive content is implicit rather than explicit,
also conforms to the Romantic style.

It should, by now, be apparent that there is a structural identity
between two social and political stereotypes and two opposing positions
in the philosophy of science. It is now necessary to show that the two
stereotypical social ideologies correspond to positions taken by real
historical actors. This will be tackled in the next section. It will
provide an opportunity to bring out further points of connection between
the social and epistemological positions, connections which reside in
matters of detail and content rather than structure. Once this has been
done, the crucial question becomes: why is it that there is an iso-
morphism between a tradition of ideological dispute and an
epistemological debate?

THE HISTORICAL LOCATION OF THE IDEOLOGIES

It is relatively easy to locate the Enlightenment and Romantic stereotypes in the pronouncements and positions of historical actors and groups.
This is because the stereotypes frequently correspond to the two basic
responses of acceptance and rejection that were available to men in
coming to terms with the major social events of the late eighteenth, the
nineteenth and early twentieth centuries. The stereotypes were
frequently elaborated as responses to wars and revolutions, to the
process of industrialisation and the nationalist strivings of Europe's
recent past. Such events are obviously divisive. They automatically
produce a polarisation of opinion because some people stand to lose and
others to gain. When their fortunes and interests are involved men's
minds will be prodded into conscious reflection and advocacy. Cases
will be argued; intellectual traditions will be ransacked in the search for
resources; moral standards of wide appeal will be invoked and structured
to suit the purposes at hand. Notions of God, Man and Nature will be
used to explain the experiences which men are undergoing and to justify

the positions in which they find themselves or the actions they are
inclined to take.

One of the major occasions for the statement of the two opposing
ideologies that I have outlined was, of course, the French Revolution of
1789.   The Revolution's individualistic and rationalistic ideals are
evident in much of the legislation that it brought to pass.   For example,
it swept away institutional arrangements such as guilds and corporations
which mediated between groups of individuals.   The structures which
articulated the social whole were broken and atomised.   Nisbet (1967)
quotes the Loi Le Chapelier of 1791 which stated: 'There is no longer any
corporation within the state; there is but the particular interest of each
individual and the general interest...' (p.36).   The crucial unit of the
family was likewise conceived by the revolutionary ideologists and
legislators as a microcosm of the Republic itself.   It was decreed that
egalitarian principles and rights should obtain in place of the autocratic
rights of the father which had previously been backed by law.
Simplification of administrative units, rationalisation of laws and govern-
ment, were the order of the day.

It was against these alarming and ultimately bloody tendencies that
the reactionary thinkers of Britain, France and Germany produced their
rhetoric and analysis.   Edmund Burke is perhaps the supreme example
with his brilliant 'Reflections on the Revolution in France' (1790).   To
those who would invoke natural law to justify our rights and freedoms,
Burke opposed an equally natural right to be governed and restrained and
to exist within a stable society.   To those who would appeal to the natural
light of reason as a basis for criticising society Burke boldly declares
that society is and must be based on prejudice not reason.   Reason as an
individual resource is inadequate.   The reason on which we do, and must,
depend is the socially embodied wisdom of our society, what in modern
parlance would be called its 'norms'.   Thus:

> We are afraid to put men to live and trade each on his own private
> stock of reason; because we suspect that the stock in each man is
> small, and that the individuals would do better to avail themselves
> of the general bank and capital of nations and ages (p.168).

Prejudice has the inestimable advantage over the calculating reason of
the individual that it is attuned to action and that it creates continuity.
Thus:

> prejudice, with its reason, has a motive to give action to that
> reason, and an affection which will give it permanence.   Prejudice
> is of ready application in the emergency; it previously engages
> the mind in a steady course of wisdom and virtue, and does not
> leave the man hesitating in the moment of decision, sceptical,
> puzzled, and unresolved.   Prejudice renders a man's virtues
> his habit; and not a series of unconnected acts.   Through just
> prejudice, his duty becomes a part of his nature (ibid).

The desire to criticise, to discuss and argue about everything, is seen
by Burke as the misfortune rather than, as his opponents could think, the

glory of his age.   To 'the whole clan of the enlightened' politicians and
literary men Burke throws out the charge that they are 'inexpiable war
with all establishments', and asserts that:

> With them it is a sufficient motive to destroy an old scheme of
> things, because it is an old one.   As to the new, they are in no
> sort of fear with regard to the duration of a building run up in
> haste; because duration is no object to those who think little or
> nothing has been done before their time, and who place all their
> hopes in discovery (ibid).

One of Burke's most interesting themes concerns simplicity and complexity and its connection with the nature of the rules which should govern
human conduct.   Man's nature and circumstances are held to be intricate.
Those who seek to produce simple laws to govern men's affairs are
grossly ignorant of their trade or negligent of their duty.   For example,
consider man's liberties and restrictions.   Because these 'vary with
times and circumstances, and admit of infinite modifications, they
cannot be settled upon any abstract rule; and nothing is so foolish as to
discuss them upon that principle' (p. 123).   Clearly Burke exemplifies
many of the facets of the Romantic style of thought.   Those who are
looking for ways of criticising Popper's conception of science could
easily borrow from Burke's position, with its reactionary scorn for discovery, its stress on complexity and rejection of simplicity, with the role
it gives to prejudice (so similar to Kuhn's idea of dogma), with its
concern for concrete action rather than abstract thought, with its theme
of social cohesion to oppose the stance of divisive, critical individualism.

The rejection of the values of the French Revolution was not
confined to Britain.   Elaborations of reactionary theory are provided by
many German thinkers - such as Müller, Haller and Möser.   They were
localists, traditionalists, patriots, monarchists and authoritarians.
Adam Müller was influenced by Burke and is a particularly interesting
case.   Selections from his 'Elements of Politics' (1808-9), have been
translated in Reiss (1955) and bring out the following points.   It is a
typical feature of Enlightenment thinkers to divide and distinguish.   Thus
they divide values from facts, man's reason from his society, his rights
from his traditions, the rational from the real, the true from the merely
believed, the public from the private.   It is a Romantic tendency to
assimilate what the Enlightenment thinker keeps apart.   Within a few
pages Müller systematically blends and unites all of these categories and
undoes all the work of boundary drawing and partitioning that is the hall-
mark of Enlightenment 'clarification'.   But what is involved here is more
than a mere tendency to divide opposed to an equal and opposite tendency
to unite.   In thought the Enlightenment habit is to distinguish, and in
thought the Romantic unifies by analogy.   In practice the Romantic takes
for granted the structural division of society, and in practice, the
Enlightenment thinker breaks them down into an atomised homogeneity.

Müller's treatment of the relations of the private sphere to the
public sphere provides an example of this - and a marked contrast to

typical utilitarian sentiments.   He says,
> The State is the totality of human affairs, their union into a
> living whole.   If we exclude for ever from this association even
> the most unimportant part of the human being, if we separate
> private life from public life even at only one point, then we can
> no longer perceive the state as a phenomenon of life, or as an
> idea... (p. 157).

The significance of this in the present context is that it illustrates the
central Romantic idea of the part or element of a system being in a
state of intimate unity with the whole.   Thus scientific conjectures are
not isolated units of thought but, as it were, microcosms of the paradigm
of which they are a part.   Or, to draw the parallel in another way, the
idea or inspiration behind a conjecture is not part of the private life of
the scientist.   It should not be seen as falling into the realm of
psychology rather than science, or be confined to an artificial 'context of
discovery' rather than the 'context of justification'.   Rather, the process
of creation is an integral part of the scientific enterprise as a whole and
should not be separated from it by an abstract principle of demarcation.

Müller goes on to apply his unifying approach to the relation of
knowledge to society, or as he puts it, science and the state.   These
should be one, like the soul and the body.   Müller insists that,
> we are not able to understand science and the intrinsic nature of
> science, if an absolute boundary is drawn between the ideal and
> the real possessions of the earth, and if only one half, the ideal
> is alloted to us.   We cannot do so if the great, whole and simple
> world is cut into two eternally separate worlds - into the actual
> world of the state and the imagined world of the sciences; for we
> remain human beings after all who are themselves whole and of
> one plane, and therefore demand a whole world which is, at it were,
> cut out in one piece (p. 156).

These examples give some idea of the detailed form taken by Romantic
thinkers on general social issues.   Another exceedingly important
battleground where the two opposing ideologies confronted one another
was, and is, economic theory.

Enlightenment thinking is very strongly represented in economics
by the advocates of laissez-faire and the classical economists of Adam
Smith and Ricardo's school.   Perhaps the most explicit statement of
their presuppositions is provided by the work of Jeremy Bentham.   As
one commentator on Bentham's economic theories has put it, 'Bentham
and the Ricardians had a common ideology' (Stark (1941 and 1946)).   All
the quotations from Bentham which follow have been taken from these
useful articles.   As Bentham himself said: he was the spiritual father
of James Mill and hence the spiritual grandfather of Ricardo.   Bentham
aligned himself wholeheartedly with Adam Smith's doctrines except when
he felt that Smith shrank from the logical consequences of his own
position.

For example, in his 'Wealth of Nations' (1776) Smith qualified his

general advocacy of free, individual bargaining in market matters by
accepting that there should be a legal restraint on the maximum rate of
interest at which money could be borrowed. Without such a limit
Smith thought that the greater part of the money which was lent would
go to 'prodigals and projectors'. Bentham's reply was, in effect, to ask:
so what? Without 'projectors' there would be no progress; risk taking
is of the essence of economic activity and the creation of wealth. This
sentiment, of course, is identical to the Popperian sentiment that
intellectual risk taking is of the essence of scientific activity and the
creation of knowledge. Bentham insisted that men must calculate for
themselves the gains and losses and risks associated with any course of
action. He claims that, 'With few exceptions, and those not very considerable ones, the attainment of the maximum of enjoyment will be most
effectually secured by leaving each individual to pursue his own maximum
of enjoyment.' This individualism naturally goes along with a tendency
to see the social whole as the mere sum of its atomic parts. The
arithmetical conception of the relation of the individual to society emerges
clearly when Bentham says:

> The whole difference between politics and morals is this: the one
> directs the operations of governments, the other directs the
> proceedings of individuals; their common object is happiness.
> That which is politically good cannot be morally bad; unless the
> rules of arithmetic, which are true for great numbers, are false
> as respects those which are small.

Morality for Bentham is assimilated to market processes. It is an act
of reason, and reason works by calculation, and calculation manipulates
quantities of pleasure and pain. It is 'nature' which has placed all men
under the 'two sovereign masters' pleasure and pain. Thus, 'The most
exalted acts of virtue may be easily reduced to a calculation of good and
evil. This is neither to degrade nor weaken them, but to represent
them as the effects of reason, and to explain them in a simple and
intelligible manner.' The stress on reason, calculation, simplicity and
intelligibility are all central themes of what I have called Enlightenment
thought. Bentham acknowledges that this rationalistic picture is an
abstraction, but holds it to be a necessary one.

The theories of classical economics eventually blossomed forth
into a full ideology usually dubbed 'social Darwinism'. This view took
up the basic economic picture of individual competition and associated it
with the 'natural' necessity for struggle, individual effort, the importance
of the survival of the fittest and the elimination of the weak and in -
efficient. The beautiful irony of this ideology was that the social order
which sought its justification in this Darwinian vision of the natural order
was itself the inspiration of the biological theory. It was through their
reading of Malthus that both Darwin and Wallace came upon the central
concept of the survival of the fittest. This concept was originally part
of the debates within political economy concerned with poor relief and
whether the conclusions to be drawn from Smithean economics were

optimistic or pessimistic (Halévy (1928), Young (1969)). Popper's
theory of ruthless refutation is social Darwinism in the field of science -
an affinity which is elaborated in his later work.

The theories of classical economics did not go unchallenged.
Britain's economic supremacy in the nineteenth century was keenly felt
by Germany who was increasingly her competitor. German thinkers
rapidly came to see Adam Smith's economic theories as intellectual
justifications for precisely those conditions which favoured Britain,
namely free-trade. Germany's perception of her own interests suggested
the opposite policy of protection. Many of her economists concluded that
abstract, universal, economic theories ought to be replaced by a style of
analysis which paid due attention to the different economic conditions of
different times and places. Thus was born the 'historical school' of
economics comprising of famous economists such as Roscher,
Hildebrand, Knies and Schmoller. Their historical principles conform
neatly to the Romantic stereotype. Economics should be a branch of
history and sociology, it should place economic activity in its social
context and not treat it in an abstract and universal way (cf Haney (1911)
who is the source of the quotations below). Wilhelm Roscher (1817-94)
outlined the programme of the historical school like this:

i   Political economy is a science which can only be explained in the
     closest relation to other social sciences, especially the history of
     jurisprudence, politics and civilisation.

ii   A people is more than a mass of existing individuals, and an invest-
     igation of its economy cannot therefore be based upon a mere
     observation of present day economic relations.

iii In order to derive laws from the mass of phenomena, as many
     peoples as possible should be compared.

iv   The historical method will be slow to praise or blame economic
     institutions.

Contrast this with the statement of a contemporary British economist
that Haney gives. 'Political economy belongs to no nation, it is of no
country; it is founded on the attributes of the human mind, and no power
can change it' (p. 10).

It would be too simple to see the polarity of economic thought
presented above as corresponding precisely to the difference between
German and British interests. There were German followers of Smith,
although they were a minority and the historical school dominated the
universities. Conversely there were British critics of the classical
school, for example the Irish economists J. Kells Ingram (1824-1907)
and Cliffe Leslie (1825-82). Indeed in Britain there was a long-standing
opposition to the growth and excesses of industrialism and its ideology
of laissez-faire. An early spokesman was the poet Samuel Taylor
Coleridge. Later the powerful rhetoric of Thomas Carlyle was un-
leashed against the socially divisive ideology of individualism with its
inhuman, mechanical overtones. (On Carlyle and the Germano-
Coleridgeans see Mander (1974)).

Jurisprudence and legislation were further fields in which exactly the same ideological polarity between Enlightenment and Romantic styles made itself felt.   Against Burke's stress on the concrete and the particular Bentham could say: 'Legislation, which has hitherto been founded principally upon the quicksands of instinct and prejudice, ought at length to be placed upon the immovable base of feelings and experience'. Bentham's watchword was 'codification'.   His desire was to place the law on a footing which was clear, simple, rational and cheap.   With the spread of French influence through Napoleon's conquests more and more of Europe was brought under the sway of legal 'codes'.   This provoked a nationalistic response, which, with Napoleon's downfall, expressed itself in the 'historical' approach to law - the approach which was referred to by the economist Roscher as one of the models for economic methodology.   Law must come from the spirit of the people; it must be national not cosmopolitan; it must be concrete case-law, not abstract codified law.   Thus Adam Müller again: 'Anyone who thinks about the law thinks immediately of a certain locality, of a certain case where the law applies... Anyone who knows a positive law in the form in which it stands in writing has merely the concept of the law i.e. nothing but a lifeless word.'   Perhaps the most famous advocate of law as an expression of the 'Volksgeist' was Carl von Savigny who conducted a debate over this question with the Heidelberg jurist Thibaut.   The issue was whether Germany should have a German Code.   Savigny opposed the idea on the grounds that previous codes in Prussia and Austria had failed.   All law should arise from customary law.   It is created by usage and popular belief, and can only be understood as a complex, historical phenomenon (cf. Montmorency (1913) and Kantorowicz (1937)).

The opposition of Enlightenment and Romantic styles is also apparent in moral theory.   The utilitarian morality of the 'philosophical radicals', Bentham, the Mills, and Sidgwick, was fiercely opposed in the late nineteenth century by the British Idealists, F.H. Bradley and Bernard Bosanquet.   Bradley's famous 'Ethical Studies' (1876) pours scorn on the idea that action can be based on calculations or derived from abstract utilitarian principles.   This simply leads to hypocrisy. Nor are moral principles universal: variation is of the essence of morality.   Nor is the same behaviour appropriate for all peoples, times and places.   It is a matter of socially varying custom and habit and it is grounded in one's station and duties.   Again, in the 'Philosophical Theory of the State' (1899), Bosanquet attacks Bentham and his individualistic account of political obligation.   Bosanquet revives Rousseau's notion of the 'real will' of a society to oppose to the idea that will is an individual and hedonistic phenomenon.   The real will is what men hear speaking to them as the voice of conscience: their better selves.   That which is higher and constraining in the individual genuinely comes, in Bosanquet's theory as in Durkheim's, from something which is external to the individual and greater than him.   Both thinkers locate that greater entity in society.   For Bosanquet, however, society is still suffused with theological overtones as Durkheim's theory would predict.

War propaganda provides another occasion for the two ideologies to raise their heads.   For example German propaganda in 1914 was steeped with stereotyped oppositions: German 'Kultur' versus English and French 'Zivilisation'; the values of Hawkers and Heroes ('Händler und Helden') and vulgarised versions of Tönnies' distinction between 'Gemeinschaft' and 'Gessellschaft' (cf. Staude (1967)).   On the other side, anti-German sentiment and avowals of individualism are fused together in a very open way by the psychologist McDougall in the preface to his book 'The Group Mind' (1920).   McDougall was highly critical of writers such as Bosanquet whose Hegelian and hence German values are scornfully dismissed.   The influence of Idealism at Oxford, says McDougall, has been 'as detrimental to honest and clear thinking as it has proved to be destructive of political morality in its native country' (p. ix).   To those who wish to see exposed 'the hollowness of its claims to all men for all time' the reader of 1918 is referred to Professor L.T. Hobhouse's 'The Metaphysical Theory of the State' (1918).   A modern reader, of course, could turn to 'The Open Society and its Enemies' (1966) with the same end in view.   This too was written to defend the values of individualism and was conceived by Popper as part of his war effort on behalf of the allies.

This brief survey has shown the systematic and pervasive character of the ideological opposition between two sets of values and two styles of thought.   The opposition was not, of course, static.   The balance of power between the contending images varied over time and from place to place.   Economic liberalism was in the ascendency in England in the mid-nineteenth century and suffered a decline in the 1870s and 80s when protectionist policies became general in Europe. Philosophical Idealism in this country arose, it seems, along with protectionism and declined after the Great War.   Nor is the connection between individual thinkers and the two stereotypes a simple one.   The stereotypes were frequently used in polemics, but of course polemic seeks out the typical or the pure case.   Thus Burke was an economic liberal but a political conservative.   He adopted utilitarianism but gave it a conservative employment.   Bentham likewise started as a political conservative opposed to the idea of natural rights.   Men had no natural rights only rights granted to them by constitutions written by legislators like himself.   On the other hand, Bentham argued from his own chosen premises to conclusions which were essentially the same as those reached by using the rhetoric of natural rights.   Individuals follow their own idiosyncratic routes to collective conclusions.

The stereotypes represent typical groupings of ideas, groupings which certainly seemed real to those who opposed them - even if their advocates were more qualified and fastidious.   Individual thinkers can be seen as selecting their own personal sample from the ideas which existed around them as cultural resources, available from the writing and rhetoric of their contemporaries and predecessors.   Over time these resources became elaborated into the two massive, characteristic styles of thinking about society which I have outlined and illustrated.

To supplement the summary of structural similarities between Popper and Kuhn on the one hand, and on the other hand the Enlightenment and Romantic ideologies, I shall briefly state some similarities of content in order to reveal their underlying social metaphors.　(i) The antithesis of individualistic democracy and collectivist, paternalist authoritarianism is apparent in the two theories of knowledge.　Popper's theory is anti-authoritarian and atomistic; Kuhn's is holistic and authoritarian.　(ii) The antithesis of cosmopolitanism and nationalism is also easy to detect.　Popper's theory of the rational unity of mankind and the 'free-trade' of ideas contrasts with the closed intellectual state of the paradigm and with the special richness of its unique language. (The parallel here is with Fichte's closed commercial state cf. Reiss (1955), and with Herder's account of language cf. Pascal (1939), both of which are components of the Romantic ideology).　(iii) The antithesis between the Benthamite lust for 'codification' and clarity and Burke's claims about the role of prejudice corresponds to the difference between Popper's methodological legislation and boundary drawing and Kuhn's stress of dogma, tradition and judgment.

The question, now, is why this repeated pattern of ideological conflict crops up in an esoteric area like the philosophy of science? Why does the philosophy of science replay these themes?　Some explanation must be sought: it is too prominent and too suggestive a connection to ignore.

THE LINK BETWEEN EPISTEMOLOGICAL
AND IDEOLOGICAL DEBATES

What has been shown so far is that there is a close similarity of structure and content between two important epistemological positions and a sequence of related ideological debates.　The hypothesis that has already been advanced to predict and explain this similarity is that theories of knowledge are, in effect, reflections of social ideologies.　It is the mechanics of the transfer of the ideas from the one realm to the other which remains to be examined.

It is not difficult to make plausible conjectures.　The ideological opposition is widely diffused through our culture.　It is a prominent and repeated pattern, so any reflective person is going to encounter it - whether through reading history books, novels or newspapers, or in responding to the rhetoric of politicians.　The pattern may not be encountered as a stark, fully articulated opposition.　It may come first through experience of one side of the polarity, then through the other, implicitly here, explicitly there, partially in this context, more fully in another.　Through the steady rhythm of social experience, and the mind's search for structure and pattern, the two archetypes will settle down in each of us and form a foundation and resource for our thinking.

To learn these ideological stereotypes we may need no more than a full exposure to our language. The meanings of words are inseperably charged with associations and connotations. These form patterns, holding together some ideas and experiences, repelling and disassociating others. Raymond Williams's book 'Culture and Society' (1958) is particularly relevant. He investigates the changing meaning of the word 'culture'. This used to refer simply to the growing or cultivation of crops, and still has these connotations. The metaphor of organic growth with its agricultural overtones made it appropriate for use by the tradition of thought stemming from Coleridge which lamented the growth of industrialism and individualism. If we introspect on the meaning which the word 'culture' now has for us it is immediately clear that it has connotations of tradition, unity and spirituality or loftiness of some form. The very notion of culture already contains in embryo the ideas which can be filled out into the Romantic image of society. This is not, of course, because that ideology has been derived by exploring the entailments of this concept. Rather, the concept now has these implications because of its association with that ideology. The logic of the concept is a residue of its social role, not vice versa. Conversely one cannot think of the word 'culture' without tacitly relating it to its antithesis. This will be something which shatters tradition and stands for change and activity. It will be something which undermines unity, suggesting division, conflict, struggle and atomisation. The antithesis must be opposed to spirituality and what is higher, suggesting worldliness, practicality, utility and money. What can this be but the image of industrialisation, the ethics of capitalism, and laissez-faire competition? In short, do we not already have in our minds, from experience of our social life and language the very social archetypes that appeared to be working their effect on the theories of knowledge just considered?

The connection between social ideologies and theories of knowledge is no mystery at all but an entirely natural and commonplace consequence of the way we live and think. The social ideologies are so pervasive that they are an obvious explanation of why our concepts have the structures that they do. Indeed the tacit employment of these ideologies as metaphors would seem almost impossible to avoid. Our familiarity with their themes and styles means that the patterns of ideas that we have picked up from them will have an utterly taken-for-granted character. They will be unconsciously embedded in the very ideas with which we have to think. What may feel to the philosopher like a pure analysis of these concepts or a pure appeal to their meaning, or the mere drawing out of their logical entailments, will, in reality, be a rehearsal of certain of the accumulated experiences of our epoch.

ANOTHER VARIABLE. KNOWLEDGE UNDER THREAT

So far the discussion of the Popperian and Kuhnian accounts of science have been entirely symmetrical.   Both have been presented as standing squarely on their respective conceptions of society.   But this very symmetry requires comment because it has implications for the Durkheimean theory as it has been elaborated so far.   If knowledge is tacitly endowed with a sacred character, because of the connection of images of knowledge to images of society, then both the Kuhnian and Popperian programmes would be equally opposed to the sociology of knowledge.   The fact is they are not equally opposed.   Indeed one of the main complaints of those influenced by Popper is that Kuhn's account is basically a piece of sociological history.   It is precisely because of this feature of Kuhn's position that the objections of subjectivism, irrationalism and relativism have been pressed upon it.   So my Durkheimean explanation of the sources of opposition to the sociology of knowledge must be incomplete.   It predicts symmetry where there is asymmetry.   There is another important variable.   This is the extent to which knowledge and society are felt to be under a threat.

Before looking at the operation of this variable I want to draw attention to how very plausible it is to expect that both approaches to knowledge would equally oppose the scientific study of science.   Both styles of thinking about knowledge are symmetrical in their potential for mystifying knowledge so as to put it beyond the reach of scientific study. The strategies for securing this end, the natural lines of retreat and defence, are of course rather different in each case.   The mystifying resources of Kuhn's account are clear because of its similarities to Burke's position.   The Romantic means of fending off unwelcome investigation into society, whether scientific or otherwise, is by stressing its complexity, its irrational and incalculable aspects, its tacit, hidden and inexpressible features.   The Popperian style of mystification is to endow logic and rationality with an a-social and, indeed, transcendent objectivity.   Thus in his recent work Popper talks of objectivity as forming a 'world' in its own right, to be distinguished from the world of physical and mental processes.   His methodological boundaries have become metaphysical and ontological distinctions (cf. Popper (1972). For a discussion, criticism and sociological reformulation see Bloor (1974)).

On the other hand, both styles of thought are capable of being harmonised with a perfectly naturalistic approach.   The sociological and factual character of Kuhn's work is frequently remarked upon - although usually as a prelude to its criticism.   The naturalistic potential of the family of theories to which Popper's work belongs is not perhaps as easy to see.   The individualistic character of Enlightenment thinking suggests that a naturalistic development of it would lead into psychology.   A comparison which reinforces this suggestion lies in the similarity of Popper's theory to classical economics.   Going back to the early utilitarians it is clear that their model of a rational, calculating, 'economic man' was a very close relation to their psychological picture of what may be called 'hedonist man', whose calculations of pleasure and pain were mediated by the rules of associationist psychology. Further it has frequently been observed how close 'associationist man' is to 'behaviourist man'. The association of ideas is very similar as a mechanism to the conditioned reflex and the stimulus-response links of behaviourist theory. The extreme outcome of this series of historical links is, perhaps, the psychologist B. F. Skinner. Skinner's hard-headed behaviourism is completely naturalistic. All behaviour whether it be of pigeons in a laboratory or a human engaged in logical reasoning is to be investigated by the same methods and explained by the same theories. Although this form of psychological theory is individualistic in its ancestory and many of its overtones there is no necessary incompatibility with a concern for social processes. Society,as Skinner makes clear, is the source of crucial 'reinforcement schedules' which mould behaviour. It therefore has a priority, from some points of view, over the individual (1945). Social patterns may have to be built up by the psychologist from individual elements, but equally those who start from social wholes have the obligation to ensure that their theories reach down to the individual level. It is a matter of preferred direction.

It may be objected that to see psychology as a naturalistic form of Popper's theory is very implausible. What about his well known hostility to 'psychologism'? My point, however, does not concern Popper's own preferences. What is at issue is the direction adopted by the root form of the theory when it is developed naturalistically.

The conclusion is that the Enlightenment or Romantic ideas in themselves do not determine their employment for or against the sociology of knowledge. For they do not, in themselves, determine whether they shall be given a naturalistic or a mystified reading. The factor which determines their direction of employment is nevertheless still derived from their underlying social models. It depends on whether the underlying social image is that of a threatened society or a stable, confident and enduring one; whether society, or some section of it, is felt to be in decline or in the ascendency.

The law which is at work here appears to be this: those who are defending a society or a sub-section of society from a perceived threat will tend to mystify its values and standards, including its knowledge. Those who are either complacently unthreatened, or those who are on the ascendency and attacking established institutions will be happy, for quite different reasons, to treat values and standards as more accessible, as this-worldly rather than as transcendent.

Some examples may make this clear. Burke was writing in response to the French Revolution and in fear of its spread across the Channel. Consequently he mystified. Popper produced his 'Logic of Scientific Discovery' between the two World Wars - after the collapse of the Habsburg Empire and under the threat of totalitarian ideologies of the left and right. As would be expected he tends to make his values and boundaries timeless and transcendent. Kuhn on the other hand betrays no hint of anxiety about the status or power of science. This is a manifest difference between the writings of the two authors that cannot fail to impress itself on any reader of their works. The early utilitarians who were aggressively critical of the 'vested interests' of established institutions were prone to be quite naturalistic. Even their rationalism had a psychological character to it. James Mill wrote his 'Analysis of the Human Mind' (1829) in order, as he put it to make 'the human mind as plain as the road from Charing Cross to St. Paul's' (Halévy (1928), p.451). The suggested law of mystification can be represented in an idealised way in Figure 3.

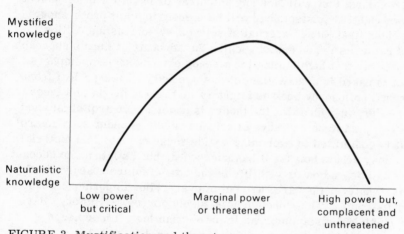

FIGURE 3 Mystification and threat

There is a natural corollary to the proposed law. This concerns the relation between the ideologies of established and dissenting groups. If an established group possesses a Romantic ideology and it is being threatened by a rising group this would make Enlightenment concepts natural weapons to select. Here the Enlightenment style would be relatively naturalistic and the Romantic style reified. Conversely, in order to criticise an establishment that uses an Enlightenment ideology some variant of Romanticism may naturally suggest itself. Thus there are naturalistic Romantic revolutionaries and reactionary Enlightenment ideologies. This explains why critics of industrial capitalism both from the left and the right have all used arguments which resemble the pro- foundly conservative Burke. It also explains the apparent oddity of why the student 'militants' of the late 1960s could subscribe to Kuhn's conception of science despite its profoundly conservative overtones. (Kuhn's critics, who have not failed to exploit this fact, appear to think

that there is an intrinsic connection between ideas and their use instead
of a historically varying one.)

THE LESSON TO BE LEARNED

The conclusion to the last section was that the variable of perceived
threat operating upon underlying social metaphors explains the differential tendency to treat knowledge as sacred and beyond the reach of
scientific study.   I now want to examine the consequence of adopting a
mystifying strategy and ways to evade its influence.

The claim that I want to put forward is that unless we adopt a
scientific approach to the nature of knowledge then our grasp of that
nature will be no more than a projection of our ideological concerns.   Our
theories of knowledge will rise and fall as their corresponding ideology
rises and declines; they will lack any autonomy or basis for development
in their own right.   Epistemology will be merely implicit propaganda.

Consider first Kuhn's account of science, which, as his critics
stress, is naturalistic and sociological.   An advocate of Kuhn's approach
could rightly say that highlighting the already obvious social metaphors
on which it is based is no criticism of that account.   Taking a leaf from
a conventional philosophy book he might argue that the origin of a theory
does not matter, provided that the theory is under the control of fact and
observation.   And Kuhn's picture of science surely is under such control
because it is committed to explaining a wide range of historical material.
Historians may debate how far it has succeeded, but its fate as an account
of science will depend on its viability in the face of future research.   So
its origins, whatever they are, are not of over-riding importance when
assessing its truth.   This conclusion is surely correct.   History, like
any other empirical discipline, has its own dynamic.   It may never
entirely transcend the influence of sources external to it, but it is not a
mere puppet.

The case is quite different for conceptions of knowledge which seek
to cut it off from the world and which reject the naturalistic approach.
Once knowledge has been made special in this way, then all control over
our theorising about its nature has been lost.   Accounts of knowledge
will be totally at the mercy of the fundamental social metaphors from
which they are obliged to start.   Unlike Kuhn's historical and naturalistic
account, which also begins under the influence of social metaphor, a
mystified account will be doomed to finish its life in as great a state of
bondage as it began it.

There is clearly a moral in this for all so-called 'philosophical'
accounts of knowledge.   Philosophy, as currently conceived, does not
have the same dynamic as empirical and historical studies, for there are
no controlled inputs of new data.   Thus there will be nothing to modify
the influence exerted by the original social metaphor.

If this claim is correct then criticism and self-criticism in philosophy are simply affirmations of the values and perspectives of some social group. When reflecting on first principles our reason very soon reaches the point where it no longer raises further questions or requires further justifications. Here the mind works on the level of what is intuitively self-evident to it - and this means depending on the taken-for-granted thought processes of some social group. Burke would call them prejudices. Of course there will be routine divergences of values in a society like ours and so one would expect standing divisions of opinion on certain philosophical matters. One would further expect the position between these contending viewpoints to be static - what variation there is in the opposing opinions will merely reflect the varying fortunes of the social ideologies which underpin the accounts of knowledge concerned. And this will be a function of what goes on outside philosophy.

If this is indeed the consequence of rejecting a naturalistic approach to knowledge then it is clear that philosophy cannot appeal to the distinction between origin and truth, or discovery and justification, in order to escape from the charge that is conceptions rest upon social ideologies. A dynamic science can ignore the origin of its ideas. But a discipline which merely elaborates and entrenches its starting point must be far more sensitive to questions of origin. Anything which hints at partiality, selectivity, limitation and onesidedness, is necessarily a reproach. It hints at error which will be ever compounded and never eliminated.

Of course these arguments are in no way decisive. They will be of no avail against a confident belief that we have access to some special source of non-empirical knowledge. They will only appeal where there is already an equal and countervailing commitment to empirical methods. To those who already have such a commitment they will suggest the desirability of accepting a naturalistic, empirical and scientific approach to the nature of scientific knowledge.

How can the fear of violating the sacredness of knowledge be overcome - or, under what conditions will it be at a minimum? The answer is clear from what has been said previously. It can only be overcome by those whose confidence in science and its methods is wellnigh total - those who utterly take it for granted; those for whom explicit belief in it is not an issue at all. This is what is conveyed in the 'Structure of Scientific Revolutions'. There, Kuhn studies something that he appears to take utterly for granted, and he studies it by methods which he takes utterly for granted. It is not unusual for historians to achieve this self-confidence. For example they often apply their historical techniques to work of past historical scholars. Thus the historian G.P. Gooch (1948) not only studied Bismark as an historical actor, he also studied the Prussian historian Treitschke, who also wrote on Bismark. The older historian is viewed as a child of his times, whose knowledge and perspective were historically conditioned just as was the statesman who was their common concern. Historians do not tremble for History when they realise that their discipline can be reflexive.

This is surely the attitude with which to approach the sociology of knowledge.   The desired stance might be called a natural, unselfconscious form of self-consciousness - though it must be admitted that this designation is grotesque.   Whatever it might be called, it can be achieved through the application of well-tried and successful routines and established techniques of enquiry.   It is the intellectual analogue of seeing society as so stable and secure that nothing will disturb or destroy it, however deeply its mysteries are probed.

The discussion of the variable of 'threat' suggested that there were two conditions under which knowledge would lose its sacred aura.   As well as the self-confident attitude just discussed there was the critical attitude of a rising group, sceptical of the knowledge of established sources of power.   This is the 'unmasking' approach which is usually associated with the sociology of knowledge.   But it has long been apparent to the more sophisticated sociologists of knowledge, like Mannheim, that this approach will not stay the course.   Scepticism will always find the sociology of knowledge useful and vice versa.   But there are profound differences between the two attitudes.   A sceptic will try to use the explanations of a belief to establish its falsehood.   He will then destroy all claims to knowledge because there is no natural limit to the scope of causal explanation.   The conclusion will be a self-defeating nihilism or inconsistent special pleading.   It is only an epistemological complacency, which feels that it can explain without destroying, that can provide a secure basis for the sociology of knowledge.

What about the fear - difficult to express but obviously very real in some minds - that the source of energy and inspiration, our conviction and faith in our knowledge, would somehow evaporate if its central mysteries are probed?   This view has grasped something important, in the way that Durkheim says a religious believer has grasped something important.   But the grasp is only partial.   A fuller analysis provides an answer to the vague anxiety.

There is indeed truth in the conviction that knowledge and science depends on something outside of mere belief.   But that outside force which sustains it is not transcendent.   There is indeed something in which knowledge 'participates' but not in the sense in which Plato said that earthly things 'participate' in the Forms.   What is 'outside' knowledge; what is greater than it; what sustains it, is of course, society itself.   If one fears for this then one rightly fears for knowledge. But as far as one can believe in its continued existence and development, then investigate knowledge as one will, it will always be there to sustain the beliefs that are investigated, the methods used, and the conclusions of the investigation itself.   And this is surely something about which it is reasonable to be complacent.

Burke had glimpsed the crucial connection, though he was anxious and not complacent.   Of learning and its sources of protection and patronage, he said, 'Happy if they had all continued to know their indissoluble union, and their proper place!   Happy if learning, not debauched by ambition, had been satisfied to continue the instructor, and not aspired to be master!' (p. 154).

It is an awareness of the indissoluble union of society and knowledge that is the answer to the fear that knowledge will lose its efficacy and authority if turned upon itself. If knowledge was a law unto itself then confusion might ensue - but the reflexive activity of science applied to itself will not dispoil the real source of energy which sustains knowledge.

I have now laid out the field of forces which operate on and within the debates over the sociology of knowledge. Ironically it is the social nature of knowledge itself which stands in the way of the sociology of knowledge, but a full awareness of that very link also provides the strength to overcome the fears that it prompts. Thus brought to light it will be easier to respond to the full range of options that are open to us and to make clear the existence of alternative ways of seeing the question at issue - in this case the nature of rationality, objectivity, logical necessity and truth.

I shall now examine the most stubborn of all obstacles to the sociology of knowledge - mathematical and logical thinking. They represent the holy of holies. Here more than anywhere else the aura of the sacred prompts a superstitious desire to avoid treating knowledge naturalistically. Both the specific arguments of the first two chapters, and the general analysis of the second two will be unconvincing unless a sociological analysis can be provided of these topics.

Chapter 5

A NATURALISTIC APPROACH
TO MATHEMATICS

In the next three chapters I shall argue that it is possible to have a sociology of mathematics in the sense of the strong programme outlined previously. Everyone accepts that it is possible to have a relatively modest sociology of mathematics studying professional recruitment, career patterns and similar topics. This might justly be called the sociology of mathematicians rather than of mathematics. A more controversial question is whether sociology can touch the very heart of mathematical knowledge. Can it explain the logical necessity of a step in reasoning or why a proof is in fact a proof? The best answer to these questions is to provide examples of such sociological analyses, and I shall attempt to do this. It must be admitted that these 'constructive proofs' cannot be offered in abundance. The reason is that mathematics is typically thought about in ways which obscure the possibility of such investigations. An enormous amount of work is devoted to maintaining a perspective which forbids a sociological standpoint. By exhibiting the tactics that are adopted to achieve this end, I hope to convey the idea that there is nothing obvious, natural or compelling about seeing mathematics as a special case which will forever defy the scrutiny of the social scientist. Indeed, I shall show that the opposite is the case. To see mathematics surrounded by a protective aura is often a strained, difficult and anxiety-ridden stance. Furthermore it leads its advocates to adopt positions at variance with the accepted spirit of scientific enquiry.

THE STANDARD EXPERIENCE
OF MATHEMATICS

It is a theorem in elementary mathematics that:

$$x(x + 2) + 1 = (x + 1)^2$$

Nobody who knows any algebra doubts the fact, and any momentary hesitation about affirming it can be overcome simply by multiplying out the right-hand side and appropriately re-arranging the terms. Once the truth of the equation has been seen it is hard to imagine what doubting it would be like. Surely nobody could both understand what was being asserted and withhold assent, in the way that someone could understand but deny the claim that Edinburgh was as far north as Moscow? Thus it seems that mathematics embodies truths which have a quite compelling nature. In this respect they are perhaps similar to common-sense truths about the familiar, material objects that surround us. They have a further property, however, which gives them a higher dignity than the deliverances of perception. Whilst we can imagine that, say, a bookcase that is in front of us might be elsewhere, we cannot imagine that the above formula might have been false - not, at least, if its symbols have attached to them the meaning which we attach to them. So the truths of mathematics are not only compelling, they are unique and unchanging. If we want an analogy it should perhaps not be the perception of things, but the dictates of moral intuition, as these were thought of in more confident and absolutistic ages than ours. What is right and proper has often seemed to men to be immediate, compelling and eternal. When struggles and perplexities were experienced these were not felt to be due to the lack of a true course of action but only to the difficulty of discerning or following it. The authority of a mathematical step as it presents itself to our consciousness is at least akin to absolute moral authority.

This standard experience of mathematics is often allied to a certain way of accounting for the development of mathematics, both in the individual and also on an historical scale. An individual confronts mathematics as a body of truth which must be mastered. There is a clear right and wrong and persistent struggle confirms the view that truths which were at first unperceived were nevertheless waiting there until the individual mind was capable of grasping them. A similar state of affairs appears in the history of mathematics. Different cultures make different and varying contributions to our present state of knowledge. All these contributions appear to be facets of one single, growing body of theorems. Whilst there clearly exist cultural differences, for example in religion and social structure, all cultures develop the same mathematics, or some preferred aspect of the one, self-consistent body of mathematics. An explanation might be given for why the Greeks developed geometry at the expense of arithmetic, whilst the Hindus did the opposite, but this is relatively uninteresting compared with the extraordinary fact that, it appears, there is no such thing as an 'alternative' mathematics.

Truly, some Reality must be responsible for this remarkable state of affairs in which a body of self-subsistent truth appears to be apprehended in ever greater detail and ever wider scope. It must be this Reality which mathematical statements describe and to which mathematical truths refer. It may further be presumed that it is the nature of this

Reality which also explains the compelling character of mathematical demonstrations and the unique and unchanging form of mathematical truth.   It must be admitted that the exact nature of this Reality in our ordinary thinking is somewhat obscure, but perhaps philosophers could define it with greater precision.   The true character of a variety of puzzling notions would then become clear.   Number, for instance, is an idea which is easy to work with in practical computations but is something whose real nature is difficult to describe.   In some way numbers seem to be objects and it is tempting to ask if there is such a thing as the number three.   Unfortunately this question invites contradictory answers from common sense.   The number three seems to be both a single entity whose properties are described by mathematicians and at the same time to be something which is as diverse, and often reproducible, as its multitude of occurences and uses requires.   It seems to be both one and many.   It is at this point that common sense gives up and passes the task of clarification to systematic philosophical thought.

The importance of the common sense experience of mathematics that has just been outlined is that it represents a body of facts for which any theory of the nature of mathematics must account.   That is to say: whatever mathematics is, it must be such as to present the appearance which has just been described.   The unique, compelling character of mathematics is part of the phenomenology of that subject.   An account of the nature of mathematics is not duty-bound to affirm these appearances as truths, but it is bound to explain them as appearances.   It is a notable characteristic of some philosophies of mathematics that they uncritically take over the phenomenological data and turn them into a metaphysics.   Once this move is granted then it indeed follows that there can be no sociology of mathematics in the sense of the strong programme.   What is required is a more critical and naturalistic approach.

One promising line of naturalistic enquiry into the nature of mathematics is that of the psychologist who studies how mathematics is learned.   Mathematics can be looked on as a body of skills, beliefs and thought processes into which individuals must be initiated.   Occasionally a person may gain such autonomy and skill that they are deemed to have made creative contributions to the body of accepted results - contributions which can in their turn be transmitted to others.   Such an approach, along with its associated analysis of mathematical ideas, may be dubbed 'psychologism'.

An early formulation of psychologism was offered by J.S. Mill. His ideas on mathematics were presented in his 'System of Logic' (1843). I intend to treat Mill's approach more fully and sympathetically than is usual and shall illustrate his account with some modern psychological work.

Perhaps the most celebrated attack on psychologism comes from the mathematician Gottlob Frege in his classic 'Foundations of Arithmetic', (1884).   Frege's criticisms are widely accepted as being fatal to Mill's approach, e.g. by Barker (1964), Cassirer (1950), Bostock (1974).   I

will show that they are not.   Nevertheless it will be important to
examine this controversy because Frege's criticisms do show the limits
of Mill's psychological and empiricist approach.   I shall argue that the
features of mathematics which impressed Frege can be formulated in
ways which extend Mill's naturalistic approach rather than merely block
it.   When this has been done the way will be opened for showing in subsequent chapters that sociology along with psychology can furnish an
adequate approach to the nature of mathematical knowledge and logical
thought.

J.S. MILL'S THEORY OF MATHEMATICS

For the empiricist, knowledge comes from experience, so for the consistent empiricist, if mathematics is knowledge, it too must come from
experience.   To those who would give mathematical truths an entirely
different status to empirical ones, and who would invent special
faculties for intuiting them, Mill says: 'Where then is the necessity for
assuming that our recognition of these truths has a different origin from
the rest of our knowledge, when its existence is perfectly accounted for
by supposing its origin to be the same?' (II, V, 4)
  Mill's avowed aim in his 'Logic' is to show that really the Deductive
sciences, like geometry and arithmetic are just species of the Inductive
sciences like physics and chemistry.   Thus: 'Deductive or Demonstra-
tive Sciences are all, without exception, Inductive Sciences...their
evidence is that of experience' (II, VI, 1).   Of course, says Mill, this
thesis is far from obvious and it must be verified for the science of
Numbers, algebra and the calculus.   Mill does not, in fact, offer any
such systematic verification.   At the most he gives some hints towards
this programme, but they are valuable hints nevertheless.
  Mill's fundamental idea is that we bring to the learning of
mathematics a stock of experiences about the properties and behaviour of
material objects.   Some of our experiences fall into the categories which
later make up the various empirical sciences.   For example, the fact
that hot water gives off steam, belongs to physics.   As well as these
facts about rather limited ranges of objects we also know facts which
apply indifferently to very wide ranges of things.   For example, whole
ranges of objects can be ordered and sorted; arranged in patterns and
arrays; grouped together and separated; aligned with one another; have
their positions interchanged; and so on.
  It is these wide-ranging truths about the ordering and patterning of
objects that Mill believes underlies mathematics.   The patterns and
groupings of physical things provide models for our thought processes.
When we think mathematically we are tacitly calling upon this knowledge.
Processes of reasoning in mathematics are just pale shadows of physical
operations with objects.   The compelling character of the steps and of
their conclusions resides in the familiar physical necessity of the physical

operations on which they are modelled. The wide applicability of arithmetical reasoning is due to the fact that we can, with more or less difficulty, assimilate many different situations to these models.

Mill's view emerges clearly in the following passage. Here he is criticising those who would treat numbers and algebraic symbols as marks on paper to be transformed by abstract rules. He says:

> That we are conscious of them, however, in their character of things, and not of mere signs, is evident from the fact that our whole process of reasoning is carried on by predicating of them the properties of things. In resolving an algebraic equation, by what rules do we proceed? By applying at each step to a, b, and x, the proposition that equals added to equals make equals; that equals taken from equals leave equals; and other propositions founded on these two. These are not properties of language, or of signs as such, but of magnitudes, which is as much to say, of all things (II, VI, 2).

Mill admits that it often feels as if we are merely transforming symbols on the page. Often there is no awareness of referring back to the experiences of things on which, he alleges, the whole process rests. Visions of childhood are not present to the mind when multiplying out the square of $(x + 1)$. This, says Mill, is because habit has rendered the process mechanical, so it has dropped from awareness. But he insists: 'when we look back to see from whence the probative force of the process is derived, we find that at every single step, unless we suppose ourselves to be thinking and talking of the things, and not the mere symbols, the evidence fails' (II, VI, 2).

Mill's idea has three important consequences. First it leads him to discern an inner structure and development in beliefs which from other points of view are often represented as simple and immediately apprehended. For example, the statement that one pebble and two pebbles make three pebbles represents for Mill an achievement of empirical knowledge. This achievement consists in realising that physical situations which strike the senses quite differently can, 'by an alteration of place and arrangement be made to produce either the one set of sensations or the other'. The modern reader can pursue precisely this topic in Piaget's (1952) account of children's growing sense of the equivalence of different arrangements of objects.

Second, Mill's approach is clearly related to educational ideas. Formal drill with written symbols should be discarded in favour of providing the relevant underlying experiences. These alone can endow the symbolic manoeuvres with meaning and give an intuitive significance to the conclusions reached. The educational link is made explicit when Mill says of the fundamental truths of arithmetic that they are:

> proved by showing to our eyes and our fingers that any given number of objects, ten balls, for example, may by separation and rearrangement exhibit to our senses all the different sets of numbers the sum of which is equal to ten. All the improved methods

of teaching arithmetic to children proceed on the knowledge of this fact. All who wish to carry the child's mind along with them in learning arithmetic; all who wish to teach numbers, and not mere ciphers - now teach it through the evidence of the senses, in the manner we have described (II, VI, 2).

The third consequence follows from these educational ideas. If there is a close connection between mathematics and experience then it ought to be possible to look at enlightened educational practice and find evidence in favour of Mill's analysis. It should be possible actually to see mathematical knowledge being created out of experience. It should be possible to exhibit those empirical facts which are said to act as models for mathematical thought processes. In order to do this I shall use some examples taken from the work of the mathematician, psychologist and educationalist Z.P. Dienes. Starting with his 'Building up Mathematics' (1960) Dienes has quite independently worked out a version of those 'improved methods' which the optimistic Mill referred to in 1843.

To see how mathematical operations can arise out of physical situations consider the following 'game' which Dienes (1964) describes. In deference to Mill I shall present it as a game that may be played with pebbles. Suppose we lay out on the ground ten groups of eight pebbles, and then add one single extra pebble. Now imagine keeping eight of these groups close together and moving two of the groups away to form a pair on their own (see Figure 4). We can now pick up one of the two isolated groups and use it to supply one extra pebble to each of the eight groups clustered together. In this way we can add an extra member to each of them. The remaining group of the two that were separated can then have added to it the single extra pebble that was mentioned at the beginning. This routine of disposing of one of the groups has the neat, reproducible feature of ending up with a number of groups all of which have the same number of pebbles, and where there are as many groups as there are pebbles in each group.

Here is a physical sequence of orderings, sortings, and distributions. The interesting thing about it is that it represents just one example of many similar cases which exhibit exactly the same pattern of behaviour. The point is not that the same game can be played with things other than pebbles but that it can be played with different numbers of objects in the groups and different numbers of groups. For consider: if we had groups with x pebbles per group, and provided we had two more groups than we had pebbles in each group, that is $(x + 2)$ groups, then the same pattern of partitioning and re-ordering can be carried out - again not forgetting the need for that isolated, extra pebble. By separating them, distributing one of the groups amongst the rest, and using the extra pebble to look after the remaining group the same restructuring will recur; the same game can be played. Of course if there are the wrong numbers of pebbles then they cannot be ordered and sorted in the neat way that looks like the configuration in the drawing.

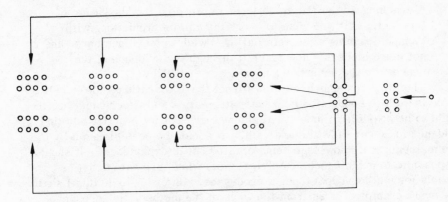

FIGURE 4 Mill's pebble arithmetic (from Dienes (1964), p. 13)

What has just been described is a physical property of material objects, namely the property that this little routine can be enacted with them. If we were to look for a shorthand way of expressing this pattern of physical relationships, what would it look like?   The answer is that a symbolic expression modelled on the experience of this game is furnished by the very equation which was presented at the beginning of the chapter as an example of a simple mathematical theorem:

$$(x + 2) x + 1 = (x + 1)^2$$

By analysing this equation Dienes shows exactly how it is underpinned by the physical operations of ordering and sorting that have just been sketched.

Dienes's analysis is this: first we have $(x + 2)$ groups of x pebbles, plus one extra pebble.   This is represented by $(x + 2) x + 1$.   These groupings can then be shifted in the way described by separating off two of the groups.   The larger number of groups consist of x squared pebbles, the isolated pair of groups consist of 2x pebbles, and then there is also the single pebble.   This process of physical re-ordering underlies the symbolic equation:

$$(x + 2) x + 1 = x^2 + 2x + 1$$

The next step in the sorting routine was to pick up one of the isolated groups and physically separate it from the other.   This is signified by:

$$x^2 + 2x + 1 = x^2 + x + x + 1$$

The group of x pebbles that has been picked up is then distributed amongst the larger collection of groups.   This distribution underlies the symbolic transformation:

$$x^2 + x + x + 1 = x (x + 1) + x + 1$$

The single pebble is then added to the remaining, isolated group.   This move can be indicated by the use of parentheses, thus:

$$x (x + 1) + x + 1 = x (x + 1) + (x + 1)$$

As Dienes points out, this sequence of moves has now produced a number of groups which all have the same number of objects in them, namely $(x + 1)$.   The number of these groups can be counted up and it will be found to be $x + 1$.   Hence it is justified to write:

$$x (x + 1) + (x + 1) = (x + 1) (x + 1) = (x + 1)^2$$

Starting from the left-hand side of the original equation it has proved possible to produce the right-hand side by a series of physical operations each one of which has been mirrored in the symbols.   The underlying physical model for at least one small segment of mathematical manipulation has thus been uncovered.   The sequence of logical moves has been produced whilst at every stage thinking and talking only of things.

Dienes ingeneously provides many other examples of a similar kind.   He gives simple routines with building blocks for doing arithmetic to a variety of different bases; for factoring quadratic forms; for solving equations; physical exemplifications of logarithms, powers,   vectors and mathematical groups; and even material and perceptual analogues of that symmetry and elegance that so subtly guides the mathematical mind. It is beside the point that physical processes are tedious compared with carrying out symbolic manipulations in a well-trained fashion.   Their point, for the purposes of the present argument, is that they provide an account of what knowledge is in fact lurking beneath the taken-for-granted symbolic procedures.   This can only be found by breaking down the smooth operation of the accomplished skill to find the empirical elements out of which it may be built.

Mill's approach is undoubtedly a promising one.   Physical objects, situations and manipulations clearly can function as models for various basic mathematical operations.   The experiences of these physical operations can plausibly be cast as the empirical basis of mathematical thought.   The search for a naturalistic understanding of mathematical knowledge would be foolish to ignore or belittle the potential in Mill's psychological and empiricist approach.   Nevertheless it is not adequate and needs to be substantially developed and extended before it can hope to do justice to mathematical knowledge.   There is no better way to bring out its limitations than to examine the intimidating treatment afforded it by Frege.

FREGE'S CRITICISMS OF MILL

Mill treats mathematics as a set of beliefs which are about the physical world and which arise out of experience of that world. The two central elements in this account are thus: (i) the beliefs and thought processes conceived as mental events, and (ii) the physical situations which the beliefs are about. Frege's criticisms accordingly have two targets of attack. He criticises the view that numbers are subjective or mental things, and also the view that numbers are either about, or are properties of, physical objects. Before looking at these criticisms a remark should be made about the values which inform them.

When Mill writes about mathematics his style is urbane, untechnical and down to earth. For him the foundations of mathematics are its psychological beginnings. They are the fundamental processes whereby the knowledge is generated and transmitted. The terms in which he thinks are more suited to the problems of the elementary mathematics teacher than the high-status professional.

Frege is completely different. To move from the 'System of Logic' to 'The Foundations of Arithmetic' is to experience a complete change of style. There is a sense of urgency and a sharp awareness of profession- al esteem in the latter work. It is imperative, the reader is told, to find satisfactory definitions for the fundamental notions of arithmetic. It is a scandal that a great science should have insecure foundations - all the more so because this permits thinkers unduly influenced by psycho- logy to misrepresent mathematics. When Frege finds himself confronted by the definition of mathematics as, 'aggregative mechanical thought' he finds it 'a typical crudity', and asserts: 'In their own interests mathematicians should, I consider, combat any view of this kind, since it is calculated to lead to the disparagement of a principal object of their study, and of their science itself along with it' (p. iv).

Frege is particularly concerned to maintain a boundary between mathematics on the one hand, and on the other the psychological and even the natural sciences. He speaks of psychological methods of argument as having 'penetrated even into the field of logic'. The consequence of this penetration, the reader is told, is that all becomes foggy and inde- finite when really order and regularity should reign. The concepts of mathematics, he avers, have a fineness of structure and a greater purity than perhaps any other science. Regarding the task of providing a secure foundation Frege asks in exasperation:

> What, then, are we to say of those who, instead of advancing this
> work where it is not yet completed, despise it, and betake them-
> selves to the nursery or bury themselves in the remotes con-
> ceivable periods of human evolution, there to discover, like John
> Stuart Mill, some gingerbread or pebble arithmetic   (p. vii).

The 'Foundations of Arithmetic' is seen today as a classic in logic. This it is; but it is also an intensely polemical work and this aspect of it tends to be imbibed and transmitted with hardly a comment.   It is steeped in the rhetoric of purity and danger, and full of the imagery of invasion, penetration, disparagement, contempt and the threat of ruin. It emphasises the distinction between the indefinite, the foggy and the confused and all that is in flux by contrast with what is pure, fine, orderly, regular and creative. It is a veritable picture of knowledge under threat. On this basis the theory proposed in chapters 3 and 4, above, would lead to the prediction that Frege would mystify and reify the concept of number and the basic principles of mathematics. The expectation is that they would be turned into mysterious but allegedly very potent objects. This is exactly what happens.

In 'Natural Symbols' (1973) Mary Douglas has drawn attention to what she calls the 'purity rule'. There is, she says, a natural tendency in all cultures to symbolise high status and strong social control by rigid bodily control. Physical eruptions and processes are framed out of discourse. The attempt is made to portray interactions as if they are between disembodied spirits. Style and behaviour are bent towards maximising the distance between an activity and its physiological origin. In my terms, invoking the purity rule would be a natural response to threat. Frege's style is a beautiful example of the purity rule in action. Indeed, he explicitly formulates it for himself (p.vii). Similarly, he expresses his contempt by locating Mill's theory in the nursery, gratuitously associating it with the process of ingestion, and flinging in a reference to evolution. It is guilty of association with physiological origins.

Why attend to the style of Frege's thinking? The point is that it gives advanced warning that his insights will be cast in terms of a vision of mathematics quite different from the naturalistic approach that is here being recommended. We shall have to be alert enough to separate Frege's insights from the standpoint in whose service they are used. They are not the exclusive property of that standpoint even though it may have inspired them. When looking at Frege's arguments the question must always be asked: can they be recast and put to work in the service of another vision of mathematics? With these provisos in mind let us turn to the critical arguments themselves.

First, consider Frege's rejection of the idea that number is something subjective, mental or psychological in nature. His argument consists in pointing out the differences between the properties of psychological entities, like experience and ideas, and the properties of mathematical notions. Our conscious states are indefinite things which fluctuate whereas the content of these states - the mathematical knowledge they contain - is definite and fixed. Again subjective states are different in different men but we want to say that mathematical ideas are the same for all.

Furthermore some very odd consequences follow from consistently treating numbers as ideas in people's minds. From the psychological point of view people do not share ideas. They are states that belong to individual minds so that an idea must belong either to your mind or mine.

Instead of saying that the number two is an idea the psychologist should therefore speak of my idea of two and your idea of two. Even this suggests an independent 'something' which is the common focus of the two psychological states, as if 'the' number two is not mental at all but the non-mental content of the mental states. A consistent psychological approach would have to insist that though we normally spoke of the number two, really all that existed was a host of individual ideas any of which could with equal justice claim to be 'the' number two. In short there would be as many number twos as there are ideas of it - a conclusion which is strikingly at variance with the usual way of regarding matters.

With heavy irony Frege reminds us that the multiplication of twos is not yet over. Must we not carry the further burden of all the unconscious twos, and the twos which will come into existence as new generations are born? Under this threat, then, let us hastily concede to Frege that numbers are not psychological entities in people's minds but are, in some way, independent objects of knowledge.

So far, Mill's position is not under too heavy pressure. His theory may be said to have an objective component in that arithmetic is about the general properties of objects, like those pebbles so despised by Frege. Mill comes in for more direct criticism when Frege addresses himself to the question: Is number a property of external things? Here the central argument is that number cannot be a property of things because the way things are numbered depends on how we regard them. There is no such thing as 'the number' belonging to, say, a pack of cards. There is one pack, but four suits, and so on. Frege says: 'an object to which I can ascribe different numbers with equal right is not what really has that number' (p.29). This, insists Frege, makes number different from what we normally count as the properties of things. The importance of our manner of regard shows that a thought process has intervened between the external object and the act of attributing a number to it. For Frege this drives a wedge between objects and the true location or focus of number. It means, he says, that 'we cannot simply assign the Number to it (the object) as a predicate' (p.29). When we look at the drawing of a triangle and discern that it has three vertices the three does not inhere in the drawing. So: 'The three in it we do not see directly; rather, we see something upon which can fasten an intellectual activity of ours leading to a judgment in which 3 occurs' (p.32).

Because we can vary our point of view and hence vary the number which is associated with an object there appears to be a difference between, say, the property of blueness, and the number three. Exception may be taken to the way Frege reaches this conclusion - perhaps he oversimplifies properties like blue - but it is surely a plausible one. Number is not something that is unproblematically in the world. There is something about the nature of number concepts that makes them different from how we usually think of material objects and their properties. Frege's conclusions so far will be accepted without reservation. Number is not psychological, nor is it simply given with Mill's pebbles.

There are a variety of other arguments which Frege presents against Mill's position and I shall return to them shortly.   For the moment the position is that Frege has ousted number from both the psychological and the material world.   If these two realms exhausted the range of possibilities then Frege's argument would make number a complete non-entity.   Naturally this is not how Frege saw the matter. There is a third possibility.   Apart from physical and psychological objects there are what Frege calls objects of Reason, or Concepts. These have that most important of properties called 'objectivity'.   It will pay to note very carefully the characteristics of objects of Reason, and things with objectivity.   Frege explains that he understands 'objective' to mean what is independent of our sensations, and of mental pictures built out of them but not what is independent of our reason.   The rest of his negative definition is given in the quotation which follows, along with a fascinating glimpse at a more positive characterisation. Here Frege says:

> I distinguish what I call objective from what is handleable or spatial or actual.   The axis of the earth is objective, so is the centre of mass of the solar system, but I should not call them actual in the way the earth itself is so.   We often speak of the equator as an imaginary line; but... it is not a creature of thought, the product of a psychological process, but is only recognised or apprehended by thought.   If to be recognised were to be created, then we should be able to say nothing positive about the equator for any period earlier than the date of its alleged creation (p. 35).

What is to be made of this definition of objectivity, this third option over and above the psychological and the material, and which is characterised by the examples given above?   I shall accept that Frege is completely right in his claim that mathematics is objective and in his positive and negative definition of objectivity.   What is missing, however, is an account of what objectivity actually is.   We have the definition, but what is the nature of the things which satisfy it?

FREGE'S DEFINITION OF OBJECTIVITY ACCEPTED,
BUT WHAT SATISFIES THIS DEFINITION?

An account is needed which gives substance to the specifications and examples that Frege has furnished.   What is neither mental nor physical; real but not actual; and exemplified by a notion like the equator?

To answer this question and ensure fidelity to Frege's definition it will be worth scrutinising his examples.   Starting with the equator; what status has this?   The equator is rather like a territorial boundary. These too can be called imaginary lines.   They may be specified by saying: imagine a line that runs south along the river, and then follows the edge of the forest to the east, etc.   It would be generally admitted that territorial boundaries have the status of social conventions, though this does not mean that they are 'mere' or 'arbitrary' conventions. They are in fact of intense significance for they relate in many complex ways to the order and regularity of the lives lived within them. Furthermore they cannot be changed by whim or caprice. Merely taking thought does not alter them. An individual may have right or wrong ideas about them, and they do not disappear if nobody happens to be entertaining a mental image of them. Nor are they physical objects which can be handled or perceived, though actual objects may be used as visible signs and indications of them. Finally such boundaries may be referred to when making statements about events which took place before anybody had ever thought of them.

This example suggests that things which have the status of social institutions are perhaps intimately connected with objectivity. Indeed the leap may be made to the hypothesis that perhaps that very special, third status between the physical and the psychological belongs, and only belongs, to what is social.

This hypothesis may be tested against Frege's other examples; the centre of gravity of the solar system and the axis of the earth. Can these be called social in nature? At first sight this may seem implausible, but this may be because of a tendency to do precisely what Frege warned against, namely, to mistake objective entities for physical or actual objects. Frege is surely right. The axis of the earth is not one of those actualities that are manifest in our experience like the earth upon which we walk. On the other hand we do want to assert that these things are real, because we believe that the rotating earth must have an axis, and any collection of massive bodies must have a centre of gravity. But what this insistence indicates is the fact that these notions have a central role to play in our conception of reality and in particular, in the mechanical theories which hold pride of place within it. It is vital to remember, however, that this reality is not an empirical reality but a systematic and highly elaborated world-picture. It is only tenuously connected with what can fall within anybody's experience. Two of the concepts which Frege has chosen as examples of what is objective thus turn out to be theoretical notions. But the theoretical component of knowledge is precisely the social component.

If the identification of the theoretical and the social should be challenged in this particular case it may be useful to look at another world-view, or theory, which has in it a concept playing a similar role to the axis of the earth's rotation. Medieval thought saw the world as a series of concentric spheres. At the centre of the earth was a point about which the whole universe was arrayed. Given the spherical and static image which dominated this cosmology there had to be such a point and it had to be where it in fact was: at the centre of the earth. For many men over many centuries this central point was a secure part of what they understood by reality. It was by no means a subjective matter even though, as we would insist, it did not correspond to reality. It was not, for example, a matter of individual choice or whim; it was not a psychological phenomenon in the sense that it differed from mind to mind or fluctuated like a mental state; and it was something about which people could be more or less informed.   Nor was the centre of the cosmos an actual object in the sense that people could, or expected, to see it or handle it.   It was in Frege's sense objective.   In another sense it was a theoretical concept, a part of contemporary cosmological theory.   In a third sense it was a social phenomenon, an instutionalised belief, a part of culture.   It was the received and transmitted world-view; sanctioned by the authorities; sustained by theology and morality and returning the service by underpinning them.

The conclusion is that the way to give a substantial meaning to Frege's definition of objectivity is to equate it with the social.   Institutionalised belief satisfies his definition: this is what objectivity is.

For Frege this rendering of his definition would, no doubt, be thoroughly objectionable.   If such a thing were possible, sociology would be an even greater threat than psychology to the purity and dignity of mathematics.   Frege's arguments were meant to keep mathematics undefiled, and yet, despite his fears of pollution he produced a definition of objectivity which allows a sociological interpretation.   That such an interpretation can slip through Frege's defences can only be seen as the very strongest argument in its favour.   The outcome is that we can adhere to Frege's definition of objectivity provided we see mathematics as social in nature rather than purely psychological or as the mere property of physical objects.   This conclusion may seem odd and perplexing.   It will therefore be useful to check the proposed interpretation by looking at Frege's remaining arguments against Mill.   This will then lead into the question of how Mill's theory may be modified to allow for the sociological processes which must be at work alongside the psychological ones.

MILL'S THEORY MODIFIED BY SOCIOLOGICAL FACTORS

Frege's remaining arguments mainly concern the 'matters of fact' which Mill believes correspond to numbers and mathematical operations.   The point at issue appears in the following passage.   In answer to the question: what is it that numbers belong to?   Mill says: 'Of course, some property belonging to the agglomeration of things...and that property is the characteristic manner in which the agglomeration is made of, and may be separated into, parts' (III, XXIV, 5).   Frege leaps on the words ' the characteristic manner'.   What, he demands to know, is the definite article doing here?   There is no single characteristic manner in which agglomerations of objects can be divided, so there is no justification for referring to 'the' characteristic manner.   A pack of cards can be sorted in many ways.   There are many games which can be played ordering and arranging pebbles.

Frege is right.   Mill has slipped in the definite article and his

theory provides no justification for it.   Here Mill must have been unconsciously responding to the same pressures as led Frege to insist
that numbers do not simply inhere in objects but depend on the way those
objects are regarded.   The social reading of Frege's definition of
objectivity provides a clue as to how this inadvertent and inconsistent
insight of Mill's may be blended with his basic approach.

Consider what is implied in talking about 'characteristic' ways of
ordering, sorting and displaying objects.   It carries connotations of
typical, usual or even traditional, patterns.   Someone may be able to
identify a rug as coming from a certain region of the world because of
the characteristic pattern woven into it.   Characteristic patterns or
displays are often social rather than personal entities.   What Mill has
therefore unwittingly done is to convey the idea that not any arrangements,
or any processes of ordering and sorting of objects, are relevant to their
functioning as the paradigm experiences of mathematics.   Of all the
countless games that can be played with pebbles, only some of the
patterns that can be made with them achieve the special status of becoming 'characteristic ways' of ordering and sorting them.   In exactly
the same way, all the countless possible patterns that may be woven into
a rug are not all equally significant for a group of traditional weavers.
There are norms for those who would weave carpets just as there are
norms for those who would learn mathematics.   Indeed the considerations
which help to establish the one set may not be so different from those at
work in the other.   Both appeal to an innate sense of order and symmetry,
of pleasing repetition, possibilities of neat closure and containment, and
smooth transitions and connections.

What Frege pounced upon was precisely the point at which Mill's
theory gave a hint that it required a sociological component to give order
to the manifold ways in which the properties of objects may be experienced.
Mill's language showed that he was actually responding to the social
component, but he let it slip from his grasp.   It is nothing other than the
lack of this component which exposes Mill's theory to all Frege's objections.   It is the following thought that is fundamental to Frege's position:
that Mill's theory only concerns itself with the merely physical aspects of
situations.   It does not succeed in grasping what it is about a situation
that is characteristically mathematical.   This missing component can
now be located in conventionality, typicality, and all that makes some
patterns be accorded the status of 'characteristic'.

Clearly an aura, a certain feel, surrounds the characteristic
patterns which exemplify mathematical moves and this aura can now be
identified as a social aura.   It is the effort and work of institutionali-
sation that infuses a special element and sets apart certain ways of
ordering, sorting and arranging objects.   A theory which tries to ground
mathematics in objects as such, and in no way captures or conveys the
fact that some patterns are specially singled out and endowed with a
special status, will be oddly deficient however promising its basis.   Thus
it is understandable how Bertrand Russell could write in his 'Portraits
from Memory' (1956),

I first read Mill's 'Logic' at the age of eighteen, and at that time
I had a very strong bias in his favour; but even then I could not
believe that our acceptance of the proposition "two and two are
four" was a generalisation from experience. I was quite at a
loss to say how we arrived at this knowledge, but it felt quite
different...' (p. 116).

To introduce into Mill's theory a normative component to do justice
to the characteristic ways of sorting objects in no way destroys its
fundamentally naturalistic thrust. The central idea that the behaviour
of objects provides a model for our thinking still survives. The difference
is that now not any such behaviour functions as a model but only certain
socially fixated or ritualised patterns.

There are however still some more objections to overcome. Frege
asks what experience or physical fact corresponds to very large numbers,
or indeed to the numbers 0 and 1. Has anybody ever had experiences
corresponding to $1,000,000 = 999,999 + 1$? And if numbers are the
properties of external objects why are we able to talk sensibly of three
ideas or three emotions which are clearly not external objects?

The point that Frege is making about the number 1 is that simply to
experience 'a thing' is not the same as to encounter 'the' number one,
hence the use of the indefinite article in one case and the definite article
in the other. Clearly Frege is correct about the experience of one. It
is not any random thing, but something regarded in a special way for
special purposes, and typically the ritualised purpose of counting. It
corresponds not to a thing but to anything regarded as an element in a
characteristic pattern. The number is the role and this must not be confused with whatever object indifferently occupies that role. The
experience which is associated with the number is the experience of
objects being accorded roles in characteristic patterns and partitionings
of objects.

What about the experience associated with zero? Frege triumph-
antly insists that nobody has ever experienced zero pebbles. Taken in a
certain way this is true. He then insists that all numbers, including zero
have the same status. Because zero cannot have an experience which
corresponds to it, Frege argues that experience therefore plays no more
part in our knowledge of any other numbers.

This assumption, that numbers are homogeneous in their nature, is
highly plausible. But it may easily be turned against Frege's theory and
used to help a modified form of Mill's theory. This is because the idea
that numbers have the status of roles and institutions is perhaps more
inviting in the case of zero than any other number. It is easy to think of
it as a convenient device or convention, something that was invented and
introduced rather than discovered or uncovered. On grounds of homogeneity, if zero is a conventional artefact then so are the rest of the
numbers.

Next comes the question about very large numbers. Clearly we
cannot experience the partitioning of one million objects in the same way

that we can five or ten objects. Arithmetic applies to large numbers as well as small numbers, so doesn't this imply that it must be independent of what our experience can tell us, and that its real nature must have nothing to do with experience?

There are clearly two general options in explaining the fact that experience and arithmetic only overlap to a limited extent. It can either be interpreted as Frege chooses to interpret it, in which case the small connection and correspondence of arithmetic and experience is merely fortuitous. Or it can be used to invest the limited connection of arithmetic and experience with supreme importance. Everything else must then be shown to grow out of that link. This is Mill's approach.

To meet Frege's challenge Mill's theory must show how experience can launch the ideas of arithmetic and endow them with the means of functioning in abstraction from the situation which originated them. The case of arithmetic with large numbers must be shown to be a derivative case that is parasitical upon those cases which can be directly related to empirical situations. The means of showing how such a process might work already lies at hand. It is implicit in the very idea that the patterns of objects which are within reach of our experience can function as models. For consider how models work and what happens when one piece of behaviour is modelled on another. The result is precisely to detach the derivative behaviour from that on which it is modelled. Think here of the carpet weavers. A weaver picks up the way that the pattern goes by watching and working with others. He can then function autonomously and apply and reapply the technique to new cases. He could, for example, set out to weave a carpet bigger than he had ever seen anyone weave before, but he need only have learned and practised on small ones. It is of the nature of techniques that they are like this. So an account of arithmetic can be based on experience of limited scope, provided that that experience furnishes models, routines and techniques which can be applied and extended indefinitely. There is no incompatibility between Mill's theory and an arithmetic which functions in areas that could not themselves be directly exemplified in our experience.

Frege's final objection serves to bring out a related but most important point. The problem is how, on Mill's theory, it is possible to speak of numbers of non-material things as when we say that jealousy, envy and lust are three different emotions. Thus says Frege:

> It would indeed be remarkable if a property abstracted from
> external things could be transferred without any change of sense to
> events, to ideas and to concepts. The effect would be just like
> speaking of fusible events, or blue ideas, or salty concepts or
> tough judgments (p. 31).

This issue is crucial, for construed generally it asks how Mill can account for the generality with which arithmetic can be applied.

The answer to this question must again focus on the way in which simple empirical situations can function as models. These situations must be such that all the cases to which arithmetic can be applied may be assimilated to them. For example, the reason why it makes sense to talk about three ideas must reside, on this theory, on our willingness and our ability to talk of ideas as if they were objects. Only as far as we are prepared to use the metaphor of object is our arithmetic applicable.

It is worth dwelling on this answer to Frege's challenge. It provides a good test case for the hypothesis that the application of arithmetic depends on assimilating each case to the behaviour of objects. The question is: do we really use objects as models or metaphors when we think about psychological phenomena, and do these really provide the channel through which arithmetical operations and numbers find their application to them? If there is such a tendency and it is successful even to a limited degree this will be evidence for a strong natural urge to use the metaphor of object. This is because mental phenomena are so distant in their nature from physical objects that they may be expected to yield only to the most determined efforts and the strongest tendencies to think in this way. Two examples will be given to show that this tendency to assimilate mental processes to objects does exist and work in the way that the present theory requires.

In his 'Science and Method' (1908) Poincaré gave a famous introspective account of how he made one of his mathematical discoveries. What is of interest here is not that the discovery was mathematical but rather the language he hit upon to express his mental state on one sleepless but creative night. Poincaré talks of his ideas as if they were the molecules of the kinetic theory of gases, rushing around and colliding, and even coalescing, with one another. He admits that the comparison is crude, but despite all his reservations this is how he finally chooses to express himself. In adopting the metaphor of atomism Poincaré is, of course, following a long tradition of 'psychological atomism'. The point is not whether this tradition, or Poincaré, is right. It is simply that, right or wrong, this tendency to use the metaphor exists. It can be invoked to explain what Frege thought never could be explained on Mill's theory: the application of number to ideas, and also the mechanism of its general application.

It might be objected that Poincaré's talk was loose and popular and so does not really prove anything serious about the way in which we give application to arithmetical concepts. A second, and more obviously scientific, example can make the same point and it also fits closely to the terms of Frege's challenge: how can numbers be applied to mental states?

It was the great achievement of nineteenth century psycho-physics to find ways of understanding mental processes mathematically and in particular to formulate the Weber-Fechner Law. This said that the intensity of a sensation is proportional to the log of the stimulus. The basic step in this achievement was to discover a way of segmenting mental processes so that these segments could be counted. The whole apparatus of arithmetic and ultimately the calculus could then be brought to bear to produce the mathematical formulation of the law.   The ploy that was used to get segmented and countable units was to introduce the notion of the 'just noticeable difference'.   A tone or weight was gradually increased until the change could be noticed by the subject.   The size of this just noticeable difference was found to be proportional to the size of the original stimulus.   On Mill's theory of arithmetic this segmentation process is the means of fastening the analogy of thing or object on to the subject under discussion so that the routines of mathematics can find an application.   It is a means of mapping psychical states on to countable things and hence of extending even further the metaphor of the discrete object.

If these arguments are correct then it can indeed be said that the scope of arithmetic is the scope of the metaphor of material object.   As long as we can see things as objects to which the operations of ordering and sorting can be imaginatively applied then we can number and count arithmetically.   The transition or link between arithmetic and the world is the link of metaphorical identification between initially dissimilar objects.   This is the key to the general problem of the wide applicability of arithmetic.   Mill's theory solves this problem by seeing it as a special case of the generality of any scientific theory or model.   The behaviour of simple objects which lies at the basis of arithmetic function as theories about the behaviour of other processes, and, as with the application of all theories, the problem is one of learning how to see the new situations as cases of the old or more familiar instances.   By contrast Frege's tendency to see arithmetical concepts as pure and detached from material objects creates a gulf between mathematics and the world.   No perilous bridge between different realms is required on Mill's theory for it begins life in the world and gradually grows from small empirical beginnings.   (For the role of models and metaphors in scientific thought see Hesse (1966).)

SUMMARY AND CONCLUSION

The interest of a psychological theory of mathematics is that it provides an empirical approach to the nature of mathematical knowledge.   Mill's 'Logic' furnished the fundamental idea that physical situations provide models for the steps in mathematical reasoning.   As the young Russell realised this account does not feel right.   There is something missing. Frege's objections made it clear what this missing ingredient is.   Mill's theory does not do justice to the objectivity of mathematical knowledge. It does not account for the obligatory nature of its steps.   It does not explain why mathematical conclusions seem as if they could not possibly be other than they are.   It is true that Mill's model situations possess a form of physical power.   We cannot order and sort objects at will.   They will not do everything that we may wish and to that extent they impose themselves on our minds.   This does not, however, provide them with the mantle of authority. We are still free to imagine that objects may behave otherwise than they do, but we do not feel similarly free with regard to mathematics. There is thus a similarity between logical and moral authority. Now authority is a social category and it was therefore of great significance to find that Frege's definition of objectivity was completely satisfied by social institutions. Mill's psychological theory was therefore developed sociologically. The psychological component provided the content of mathematical ideas, the sociological component dealt with the selection of the physical models and accounted for their aura of authority. The exact nature of this authority and how it works in practice will be explored in more detail in a subsequent chapter. It is a delicate and interesting matter. A sociologically extended version of Mill's theory was then found to overcome the remainder of Frege's arguments. These concerned the analysis of numbers like unity and zero. By exploiting the concepts of model and metaphor it was also possible to overcome his further arguments about the arithmetic of large numbers and its wide range of application.

In relating the modified form of Mill's theory back to the phenomenology of mathematics, there are two remaining problems, a minor one and a major one. The minor problem concerns the feeling noted earlier that some Reality is needed to account for mathematics. On the present theory this feeling is justifiable and explicable. Parts of that reality is the world of physical objects and part of it is society. But it is sometimes said that pure mathematics is 'about' a special reality, and what is intended here is some alleged 'mathematical reality'. The physical world is thus excluded as a candidate. Does the present theory therefore entail that people obscurely feel mathematics to be about society? Such a statement sounds very odd, but if mathematics is about number and its relations and if these are social creations and conventions then, indeed, mathematics is about something social. In an indirect sense it therefore is 'about' society. It is about society in the same sense as Durkheim said that religion is about society. The reality that it appears to be about represents a transfigured understanding of the social labour that has been invested in it. From the present point of view it is a most interesting and encouraging fact that the phenomenology of mathematical concepts is vague and vascillating. For example, although it is sometimes said that mathematical propositions are about a special reality they are also sometimes said to be a part of this reality. The connection or the mode of participation involved is always hinted at and never spelled out - as when Frege talks vaguely, not of numbers being concepts, but of 'discovering numbers in concepts' and of the 'transparency' of pure concepts to the intellect. In the face of such unpromising and imprecise conceptions my theory may justifiably take its stand if it captures some of the more prominent facts and suggests clear lines of development.

The more important problem concerns the uniqueness of mathematics. Little has been said about this. There is no doubt

however that on the present theory the belief that mathematics is
unique has exactly the same status as the belief that there is a unique
moral truth.   But if history demonstrates the variety of moral beliefs
does it not also demonstrate the uniqueness of mathematical truth?
Do not the facts refute the claim that logical compulsion is social in
nature?   This issue will be the topic of the next chapter.

Chapter 6

CAN THERE BE AN ALTERNATIVE MATHEMATICS?

The idea that there can be variation in mathematics just as there is variation in social organisation appears to some sociologists to be a monstrous absurdity (Stark (1958) p. 162). Stark goes on to say: 'Surely, there can only be one science of numbers, for ever self-identical in its content' (p. 162).

Only a few writers have set themselves against this apparently obvious fact. One of them, Oswald Spengler, is very little read now. His once popular 'Decline of the West' (1926) contains a lengthy and fascinating, if sometimes obscure chapter on this theme called The Meaning of Number. Significantly it occurs very prominently, right at the beginning of the book. Spengler is prepared to assert that: 'There is not and cannot be number as such. There are several number worlds because there are several cultures' (p. 59, vol. 1)

Wittgenstein is reported to have read and been impressed by Spengler's book (Janik and Toulmin (1973), p. 177). He too embraces this 'monstrous absurdity' in his sociologically oriented 'Remarks on the Foundations of Mathematics' (1956). Perhaps this explains the relative neglect of that work. Philosophers who feel at home with Wittgenstein's other writings often discern little coherence or sense in his account of mathematics (cf. Bloor (1973)).

To decide whether there can be an alternative mathematics it is important to ask: what would such things look like? By what signs could they be recognised, and what is to count as an alternative mathematics?

WHAT WOULD AN ALTERNATIVE MATHEMATICS LOOK LIKE?

Part of the answer can be given easily. An alternative mathematics would look like error or inadequacy. A real alternative to our mathematics would have to lead us along paths where we were not spontaneously inclined to go. At least some of its methods and steps in reasoning would have to violate our sense of logical and cognitive

propriety.   Perhaps we would see conclusions being reached with which
we simply did not agree.   Or we would see proofs accepted for results
with which we agreed, but where the proofs did not seem to prove anything at all.   We would then say that the alternative mathematics got the
right answer for the wrong reason.   Conversely we would perhaps see
clear and compelling lines of reasoning - compelling from our standpoint -
rejected or ignored.   An alternative mathematics might also be embedded
in a whole context of purposes and meanings which were utterly alien to
our mathematics.   Its point would perhaps seem to us to be barely
intelligible.

Although an alternative mathematics would look like error, not any
mistakes would constitute an alternative mathematics.   Some error is
best seen as a minor deviation from a clear direction of development.
The idiosyncracy of contemporary schoolboy mathematics does not constitute an alternative.   So something more than error is required.

The ' errors' in an alternative mathematics would have to be
systematic, stubborn and basic.   Those features which we deem error
would perhaps all be seen to cohere and meaningfully relate to one another
by the practitioners of the alternative mathematics.   They would agree
with one another about how to respond to them: about how to develop them;
about how to interpret them: and how to transmit their style of thinking
to subsequent generations.   The practitioners would have to proceed in
what was, to them, a natural and compelling way.

There is, of course, another way in which the stubborn errors of
an alternative mathematics could make it different from ours.   Instead
of there being coherence and agreement it could be that lack of consensus
was precisely the respect in which the alternative was different to ours.
For us agreement is of the essence of mathematics.   An alternative
might be one in which dispute was endemic.   To its adherents this lack
might be deemed to belong to the very nature of the enterprise, just as,
in many quarters, religion is viewed as being a matter for the individual
conscience.   Cognitive toleration might become a mathematical virtue.

This range of specifications is sufficient for the purposes in hand.
If anything satisfied them it would be good grounds for calling it an
alternative mathematics.

It may be objected that all that the satisfaction of these conditions
would show is that error can be systematic, stubborn and basic.
Institutionalised patterns of logical error are surely no less erroneous
than individual errors?   To see how to respond to this objection consider
the question: can there be alternative moralities?   Imagine this being
asked in an age of absolute moral confidence.   Suppose the moral code of
the time is thought to have been given by God.   This confident standpoint
clearly delineates what is right.   Any deviation must therefore be wrong -
so how can there be a so-called alternative morality?   Would it not
violate God's nature to be morally ambivalent or equivocal?

The only way of answering the moral absolutist is to say that an
alternative morality would be one in which men systematically take for

granted things that he deemed to be sinful.   They weave them together
to make a way of life which they take for granted and transmit to their
children.   An alternative morality should therefore not be likened to
criminal behaviour in our society for it would itself be the norm,
although it would come to our attention because it deviated from our
norms.   Naturally the moral absolutist would sweep this point aside by
observing that immorality on a social or national scale is still immorality.   Institutionalised sin is still sin; societies like people can be
wicked.

For the purpose of scientific investigation it is clear that this
moral standpoint must be overridden by another and different moral
imperative: the demand for a detached and general perspective.   Thus
the anthropologist will be prepared to talk of alternative moral systems
provided only that they appear to be established and engrained in the life
of a culture.   This is the characteristic that would have to be located in
mathematics if talk of an alternative is to make sense.

There is however one more complicating factor which must be
noted.   The world does not, for the most part, consist of isolated
cultures which develop autonomous moral and cognitive styles.   There
is cultural contact and diffusion.   In as far as the world is socially
blended then to that extent it will be cognitively and morally blended too.
Again, mathematics like morality is designed to meet the requirements
of men who hold a great deal in common in their physiology and in their
physical environment.   So this too is a factor working towards uniformity
and a common backdrop of cognitive and moral style.   Alternatives in
mathematics must be looked for within these natural constraints.   But,
still, that uniformity and consensus - where it exists - can be accounted
for causally.   It is not necessary to postulate any vague Mathematical
Reality.   The only realities that need be evoked are those assumed in the
modified form of Mill's theory, namely the natural and social worlds.
From the point of view of an empirical social science the issue is how the
observed pattern of uniformity and variation of belief - in whatever proportion these might appear - can be accounted for by natural causes.

I shall offer illustrations of four types of variation in mathematical
thought each of which can be traced back to social causes.   They are (i)
variation in the broad cognitive style of mathematics; (ii) variation in the
framework of associations, relationships, uses, analogies, and the metaphysical implications attributed to mathematics; (iii) variations in the
meanings attached to computations and symbolic manipulations; (iv)
variation in rigour and the type of reasoning which is held to prove a
conclusion.   A fifth source of variation will be left for the next chapter.
This is variation in the content and use of those basic operations of
thought which are held to be self-evident logical truths.

The first examples, concerning cognitive style, will contrast
aspects of Greek and Alexandrian mathematics with the corresponding
parts of contemporary mathematics.

IS 'ONE' A NUMBER?

The following statements were commonplace in early Greek mathematics:
one is not a number; one is neither odd nor even but even-odd; two is not
an even number.   Nowadays each of these claims is rejected as false.
For us, one is a number just like any other.   Frege could cite it as such
in his arguments without a second thought.   Furthermore, one is an odd
number just as two is an even number, and there is no such category as
even-odd.   So what did the Greeks have in mind?
   The reason why they said that one is not a number is because they
saw it as the starting point or generator of number.   Their meaning is
like ours when we say that a number of people went to a lecture, implying
that more than one went.   Aristotle was offering his own version of this
standard view when he said in his 'Metaphysics' (Warrington (1956), p. 281):
"one' means the measure of some plurality, and 'number' a measured
plurality or a plurality of measures. Therefore, of course, one is not a
number; the measure is not plural, but both it and the one are starting
points' (N I 1087b33).
   Occasionally an attempt was made to talk of one as if it were a
number.   Thus Chrysippus in the third century BC spoke of a 'multitude
one'.   Iamblichus rejected this as a contradiction.   Sir Thomas Heath
quoted this example in his 'History of Greek Mathematics' (1921, vol. 1,
p. 69) saying that Chrysippus's isolated view was important because it was,
'an attempt to bring 1 into the conception of number'.   It was important, in
other words, as an anticipation of our standpoint.   From the present
point of view it is perhaps more interesting as a comment on the nature of
logical confusion, for this was the charge made by Iamblichus.   What
Iamblichus saw as mere confusion we take for granted as obvious.   Perhaps
therefore what we reject as logical absurdity will one day appear to be
self-evident truth.   Perceived absurdity would appear to be a function of
the underlying classification which is taken for granted.   The standard
early Greek classification of number is clearly different from ours.
Different things will therefore count as violations of order and coherence,
and so different things will count as confusions or contradiction.
   Part of the Greek classification of number is similar to ours.   They
too sorted numbers into odd and even.   What, then, of the idea that one is
to be classed as even-odd?   This is because one generates both odd and
even numbers, so it must partake of both natures.   It stands astride and
above the odd-even dichotomy representing its origin or source.   There
are some anthropological parallels here.   Origin myths often appeal to
events which violate the very categories and classifications they are meant
to explain.   When men tell the story of their cosmos, processes like
incest are frequently invoked, as our own Adam and Eve myth shows.   One
is here being accorded a similar category-violating status.   Other
attributes of myth might therefore be expected to adhere to it as well.
This expectation will prove correct.
   Sometimes two was also denied the status of number because it was

the generator of the even numbers.   This classification, however, was
less common and certainly less enduring than the idea that unity was not
a number.

Are these points perhaps isolated curiosities which should be dismissed as mere 'quibbles'? (as by Van Der Waerden (1954)).   If the aim
is to reconstruct as much as possible of Greek mathematics in modern
terms then, indeed, the matter may not be of much concern.   On the other
hand these differences in classification may be symptoms of something
deep - of a divergence of cognitive style between Greek mathematics and
ours.   This is the view taken by Jacob Klein in his difficult but fascinating book 'Greek Mathematical Thought and the Origin of Algebra' (1968).

Klein's contention is that it is an error to see a single unbroken
tradition of meaning attached to the notion of number.   More than simple
growth has characterised the changes from Pythagoras and Plato, through
the great sixteenth-century mathematicians like Vieta and Stevin, to the
present.   His point is not that the notion of number has undergone an
extension to include first the rational numbers, then the real numbers and
finally the complex numbers.   Rather, his point is that there has been a
change in what he calls the 'intention' of number.   Thus Klein argues
that when Renaissance algebraists assimilated the work of say, the
Alexandrian mathematician Diophantus they at the same time reinterpreted it.   The continuity that we see in the tradition of mathematics is
an artefact.   It derives from reading back our own style of thought into
the earlier work.

The difference in ancient and modern number concepts that Klein
discerns is this: number for the ancients was always a number of something or other.   It was always a determinate quantity and referred to a
collection of entities.   These may be objects of perception, such as
cattle, or they could be pure units conceived by thought in abstraction
from any particular objects.   Klein argues that this notion of number is
radically different from that currently used in the processes of algebra.
Here, says Klein, number must be conceived symbolically rather than as
a determinate number of things.   It is sometimes difficult to be sure
what Klein means by 'symbolic' but the substance of the claim is clear and
important.   I shall convey Klein's point by following his discussion of
Diophantus' work.   In order to make the points as concretely as possible
I shall give some simple examples from Diophantus.   These will be taken
from Heath's (1910) translation and commentary.

Although Diophantus' chief work is called the 'Arithmetic' it is not
difficult to see why it is generally taken to be a treatise in algebra.   Here
is a typical problem from Diophantus, it is problem 9 of Bk. II.   'Divide
a number, such as 13, which is the sum of two squares 4 and 9, into two
other squares'.   Diophantus says that since the squares given in the
problem are 2 squared and 3 squared he will take $(x + 2)$ squared and
$(mx - 3)$ squared as the two squares for which he is searching and further
will assume that $m = 2$.   Now Diophantus has reduced the problem of
finding two unknown squares to that of finding one unknown quantity.   He

does this by relating the two unknowns to one another.   Then he has:

$$(x + 2)^2 + (2x - 3)^2 = 13 \quad \text{therefore } x = \frac{8}{5}$$

so the required squares are $\frac{324}{25}$ and $\frac{1}{25}$

Clearly this is a calculation of the sort that is now counted as a piece of algebra.   It has an unknown quantity and an equation is set up and manipulated to reveal the value of the unknown.   But no sooner does this point become obvious to a modern reader than certain oddities begin to strike him.   A survey of Diophantus' work quickly yields differences between his thinking and that behind contemporary elementary algebra. For example all of Diophantus' algebra consists in looking for quite determinate numbers.   The algebraic processes are not used with the same generality as we would use them.   They are always subordinated to numerical problems.   Thus in the example above quite specific assumptions were introduced in order to yield two numbers that would meet the required conditions.   Wherever the algebra yields what we would call negative numbers Diophantus rejects the original problem as impossible or erroneously formulated.   Similarly when he works on a problem which can be cast into a quadratic equation he typically only gives one of the two values which satisfy such equations.   This is done even when both of these values are positive.

Consider another problem from the 'Arithmetic', problem 28 of Bk II.   This will again bring out the differences with modern styles of thought.   'Find two squares such that the sum of the product and either is a square.'   The modern rendering of Diophantus' reasoning is given by Heath as follows.   Let x squared and y squared be the required numbers. The conditions they must satisfy are that

$$x^2 y^2 + y^2 \quad \text{and} \quad x^2 y^2 + x^2$$

be squares.   Now the first of these will be a square if x squared plus one is a square.   Diophantus then assumes that this may be made equal to (x - 2) all squared, and hence x = 3/4.   Substituting this value in the second equation means that

$$9(y^2 + 1)/16$$

must be a square.   Here Diophantus assumes that

$$9(y^2 + 1) = (3y - 4)^2$$

hence y = 7/24.   So the two required squares are 9/16 and 49/576.

This account of Diophantus' reasoning brings out the way that the whole course of the argument is subordinated to the aim of finding definite numerical values.   The most important point however is that Heath's

rendering given above is not in fact quite the same as Diophantus' own
line of reasoning. It is an updated reconstruction which casts it in a
form rather different from the original. Heath very clearly draws
attention to this fact, and in particular notes that his reconstruction proceeds by introducing two unknowns, x and y. He explains that Diophantus
only works with one unknown which was always designated by S, thus:
'We may say, then, that in general Diophantus is obliged to express all
his unknowns in terms, or as functions, of one variable' (p.52).

This comment helps to show what Klein had in mind when he said
that Diophantus is systematically reinterpreted by modern thinkers.
Notice that Heath spoke of the symbol S as a 'variable'. This suggests
that all that has happened in the reconstruction of Diophantus' argument is
that the procedure has been shortened and simplified by working with two
variables instead of one. Klein insists that Diophantus' symbol S is not a
variable at all and that to see it as such is to misrepresent one of the
presuppositions of Greek mathematics. From the Greek standpoint the
symbol S can only refer to a specific unknown number. Variables by
contrast do not stand for specific unknown numbers. As their name
suggests they stand for a whole varying range of values which obey some
rule or law.

The character of a variable as distinct from an unknown number can
be illustrated with some elementary school algebra. In school, equations
like

$$y = x^2 + x - 6$$

are either presented as, or are soon thought of as, the equation of a curve.
Here the curve looks like Figure 5.

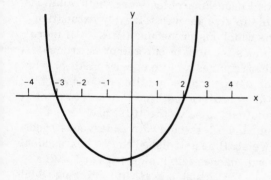

FIGURE 5

As the values of x and y in the equation vary a point satisfying it traces
out the curve. Here x and y are truly variables.

Diophantus is often concerned with problems which yield equations
rather like the above but with his symbol S for our x. To us this would
yield two values of S namely +2 and -3. He would reject the latter

solution as impossible and thus confine himself to what is, in effect, a single point on the above graph. He would be concerned with the point where the curve crosses the positive side of the x-axis. Diophantus, however, does not see his isolated value of S = +2 as being merely one value of the variable S. For him there is no context of surrounding values situated along a curved line. There is no two-dimensional space of graph paper in which the relationship of the equation traces out a curve. The unknown point for which the symbol stands is complete and entire in itself. The web of relationships existing around it that our mathematics has constructed simply did not exist for Diophantus.

Consider the negative solution S = -3, which Diophantus would reject. For us this has a vivid connection with the other value of S = +2. They are two points related together because they represent the intersection of a straight line, y = 0, with the curve of the equation. Take away this interpretive apparatus, take away indeed negative numbers, and there is nothing to hold the two points together in the way that there is for us.

In all this the difficulty for us is to learn to 'unsee' what we have been trained to see. It is the problem of imagining what it must be like for this alternative, truncated vision not to be truncated at all, but to fill the world as completely as our vision fills our world.

One way of sensing this different approach to number, this counting rather than symbolic conception, is to notice how divergent are the expect- ations and intuitions which guide a contemporary mathematician compared with Diophantus. Here is a delightful description by the historian of mathematics Hankel of his experience when reading Diophantus. Hankel begins by noticing the widely different types of problem with which Diophantus deals and the lack of any recognisable principle of grouping. He goes on:

Almost more different in kind than the problems are their solutions, and we are completely unable to give an even tolerably exhaustive review of the different turns which his procedure takes. Of more general comprehensive methods there is in our author no trace discoverable: every question requires a quite special method, which often will not serve even for the most closely allied problems. It is on that account difficult for a modern mathematician even after studying 100 Diophantine solutions to solve the 101st problem; and if we have made the attempt, and after some vain endeavours read Diophantus' own solution, we shall be astonished to see how suddenly he leaves the broad high-road, dashes into a side-path and with a quick turn reaches the goal, often enough a goal with reaching which we should not be content; we expect to have to climb a toilsome path, but to be rewarded at the end by an extensive view; instead of which our guide leads by narrow, strange, but smooth ways to a small eminence; he has finished! He lacks the calm and concentrated energy for a deep plunge into a single important problem; and in this way the reader also hurries with inward unrest from problem to problem, as in a game of riddles, without being able to enjoy the individual one.   Diophantus dazzles more than he delights. He is in a wonderful measure shrewd, clever, quick-sighted, indefatigable, but does not penetrate thoroughly or deeply into the root of the matter.   As his problems seemed framed in obedience to no obvious scientific necessity, but often only for the sake of the solution, the solution itself also lacks completeness and deeper signification.   He is a brilliant performer in the art of indeterm-inate analysis invented by him, but the science has nevertheless been indebted, at least directly, to this brilliant genius for few methods, because he was deficient in the speculative thought which sees in the True more than the Correct.   This is the general impression which I have derived from a thorough and repeated study of Diophantus' arithmetic (quoted by Heath (1910) p.54).

The important thing is how easy it is to understand Hankel's reactions without being versed in mathematics.   He is describing picturesquely but authentically a quite typical experience.   Does not Hankel capture exactly the feeling of coming into contact with odd moral, political, aesthetic or social attitudes?   Isn't it the same experience as joining an unfamiliar social group?   Moment by moment expectations are violated; our ability to anticipate breaks down; watchfulness is necessary; the events are one move ahead.   The smooth predictability of patterns of response is absent: why was this done or that said?   In part this may give rise to admiration for the unusual skills that are displayed; in part it will cause exasperation. We encounter a blindness to possibilities that are obvious to us. Hankel's account is phenomenological evidence that Diophantus' work represents mathematical thinking which is different to ours - as different as the morality or religion of another culture is different to our morality or religion.

The idea that number was a number of units, and that the unit itself had a special nature, lasted until the sixteenth century.   One mathema-tician who helped change this was the Dutchman Simon Stevin.   Some points of sociological interest emerge from looking at his arguments.

Although Stevin felt it necessary to justify the reclassification of the unit as a number he does not appear to have adopted the idea because of the arguments he adduced.   The arguments were after-the-fact defences for a position which seemed quite evident.   Klein quotes him as saying that he did not doubt that one was a number: 'no, definitely not, since I was as assured of this as if nature herself had told me with her own mouth' (p.191).   The idea, it may be assumed from this, was becoming taken-for-granted or 'natural', although there was evidently sufficient disagree-ment on the matter to make some show of argument necessary.   Stevin's argument was that if number is made up of a multitude of units, then a unit is a part of number.   The part must have the same nature as the whole, therefore the unit is a number.   To deny this, says Stevin, is like denying that a piece of bread is itself bread.

This argument might produce the conclusion to which we now adhere but it is not compelling.   It requires an initial sympathy with the idea of the homogeneity and continuity of number before its assumption about the part being the same as the whole can be granted. Stevin makes clear that these are indeed the ideas that he is working with. What he has in mind is, in fact, the analogy of number and length or size or magnitude. Thus: 'The community and similarity of magnitude and number is so universal that it almost resembles identity' (p. 194).

The new classification of number rests on seeing how number can be likened to a line, and this is precisely the analogy which is excluded by the previous stress on the discontinuous act of counting. It is doubtful if the issue between the old and the new view could have been settled by explicit argument. These would always depend on underlying judgments about the plausibility of the basic analogy between number and line. This in turn ramifies into the issue of the connection and relative priority of arithmetic and geometry.

What is it that changes our sense of the connection between the different parts of knowledge? What makes an analogy such as Stevin's natural to one person but not to another? The answer must be: past experiences and present purposes. And these must be seen both in their social setting and against a backdrop of natural, psychological propensities. What controls these fundamental mathematical analogies can be glimpsed by comparing Stevin, who advocated a reclassification of number, with those who opposed it, clinging to the Greek view.

Stevin was an engineer. The major mathematical practitioners of the time all had preoccupations which were technological or applied (cf. Strong (1966)). Their practical bias led them to use number not merely to count but also to measure. It was probably practical concerns which broke down the boundaries between geometry and arithmetic. Numbers came to perform a new function by indicating the properties of moving, active processes of change. For example number and measurement became central to an intellectual grasp of ballistics, navigation and the use of machinery.

For those who opposed the new conceptions, which Nature had whispered into Stevin's ear, number still had a more static character. Number was to be understood by being classified. Its most important properties were those in virtue of which it was assigned to its appropriate category. The relation of number to the world was certainly important to these thinkers but it was often conceived in a different way to the engineers, or was believed to have aspects over and above those stressed by the practical men. Number was a symbolic exemplification of the order and hierarchy of Being. It had metaphysical and theological significance.

In his 'Procedures and Metaphysics' (1966) Strong cogently argues that two different groups of men constituted the scientific and obscurantist party respectively. Kepler was perhaps the nearest to being a representative of both casts of mind. More recent research has stressed the connection between these groups and their attitudes, suggesting that practical and mystical views were frequently combined, e.g. French (1972). Whatever the outcome of this historical debate one general point is clear: there was a close connection between sixteenth-century technology and the new conception of number. However the transition from the older to the newer view was mediated, its general direction requires explaining and as Strong's work suggests, the growing requirements of technology provide the most plausible cause of the change.

The view that has been briefly referred to as mystical or numerological deserves closer examination. This will constitute the second example of variation in mathematical thought. It will begin with a sketch of the Pythagorean and Platonic conceptions of mathematics.

PYTHAGOREAN AND PLATONIC NUMBER

The Greeks used calculation for practical purposes in the market place, but strongly differentiated this use of number from the higher, intellectual contemplation of its properties. Very roughly this corresponds to their distinction between 'logistic' and 'arithmetic', or practical and theoretical arithmetic. This difference between two ways of knowing number corresponds to a social discrimination. Thus in the 'Philebus' Plato has Socrates say: 'Must it not first be said that the arithmetic of the crowd is one thing and that of lovers of wisdom is another?' (56 D). For Plato it is the lovers of wisdom, the philosophers, who would be the rulers in a properly ordered society.

The theoretical contemplation of number was concerned with a property called its 'eidos'. Klein explains that this refers to the 'kind' or 'species' of the number, or more literally to its 'shape', or 'look'. To see how numbers can have shapes or looks it has to be recalled that number here refers exclusively to numbers of things, and numbers of things can always be represented by numbers of dots. These dots can often be arranged in characteristic shapes, such as squares, triangles or oblongs. This makes it natural to speak of square numbers, triangular numbers, oblong numbers and so on into three dimensions if necessary. Frege would perhaps have thought that an oblong number was as absurd as an oblong concept, but the meaning is quite clear as the figures below show:

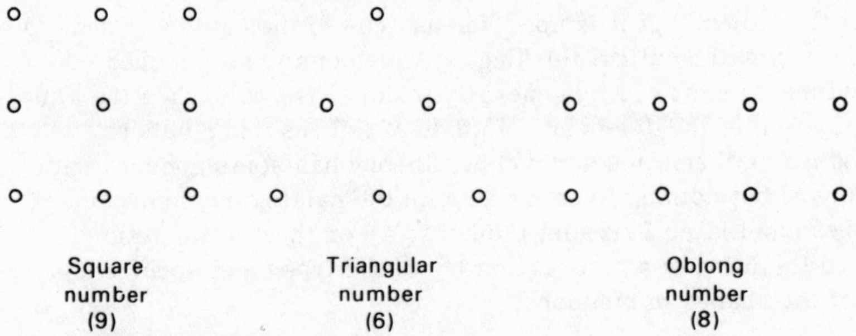

Square	Triangular	Oblong
number	number	number
(9)	(6)	(8)

FIGURE 6   Shaped numbers

Once numbers have been categorised in this way it is possible to investigate their properties as shapes. For example, successive triangular numbers give a square when added together.   The Greeks used a device called the 'gnomon'.   This was an appropriately shaped number, which, when added to one of the above shapes, did not alter the general configuration.   For example the 'gnomon' of a square number would have to produce another square number, and would therefore have to look like this:

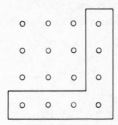

FIGURE 7   The 'gnomon' of a square number

By counting up the dots in the 'gnomon' some general properties of the configurations soon emerge.   For example every 'gnomon' of a square number is one of the sequence of odd numbers 3, 5, 7, ...   It stands out clearly that the total number of dots in any square will be equal to the sum of some sequence of these odd numbers.   A variety of such results, some of them quite sophisticated, can be achieved in this way.

The first thing that may be noticed about this approach to arithmetic is how well it fits Mill's account.   It is an historical case of the knowledge of numbers being built up by observing objects when they are subject to simple ordering and sorting operations.   Obviously some of the conclusions of Greek mathematics are likely to cross cultural and historical boundaries because they depend on experiences which anyone may have impressed upon them.

The second observation concerns not what is universal, but what is peculiar to this arithmetic.   Notice how it crystallised a certain feature of experience - the 'gnomon' - and turned it into a specialised tool of research.   Although from the point of view of our arithmetic the idea of the 'gnomon' is perfectly intelligible it is not for us a specially significant idea.   Naturally, with our greatly extended knowledge, we have ideas that play similar roles, but it is not , for us, one of the basic and central operations in our mathematical thinking.   As Klein notes: 'Indeed operations with a gnomon ... do generally make sense only when the aim of the investigation is the discovery of kinds of figures and numbers' (p.56).   Modern mathematics and number theory has some concern with kinds of numbers but nothing to compare with the cataloguing approach of the Pythagorean and later Platonist thinkers.   For them arithmetic often assumed the form of a natural history of the types and species and subspecies of the shapes of numbers.

What was the interest of this form of theoretical arithmetic?   The answer is that in arithmetic these thinkers found a classificatory scheme which symbolised society, life and nature.   Its order and hierarchy captured for them both the unity of the cosmos and man's aspirations and role in it.   The various types of number 'stood for' properties like Justice, Harmony and God.   The classification of number resonated with the classifications of daily thought and life.   Contemplation of the former was a means of grasping in thought the true meaning of the latter.   It was a way of making intellectual contact with the essences and potencies which underlay the order of things.   It might almost be looked upon as a peculiar form of 'applied' mathematics because of the intimate relation that it was held to possess to practical matters.

At its simplest level the modes of correspondence between mathematics and the world emerges in the way in which the Pythagoreans, and later the Neo-Platonists, ran together social, natural and numerical properties.   Their famous Table of Opposites reveals this alignment of their categories:

Male	Female
Light	Darkness
Good	Bad
Odd	Even
Square	Oblong etc.

In more elaborated versions of the Pythagorean vision the specific properties of numbers were often invested with meaning and studied accordingly.   For example the number ten was related to health and cosmic order.   Not only did number symbolise cosmoc forces it was also held to possess or participate in some way in divine efficacy.   The knowledge of number was thus a means for placing the mind in valuable moral states of strength and grace.

It is now possible to see the character of the opposition that Stevin's ideas were facing.   It was no small matter to treat one as being just like any other number because this would be to ignore and cut across the meanings and classifications that had been worked out.   It would tangle and confuse the intricate pattern of correspondences and analogies that connected the numbers.   Stevin was introducing a levelling and secularisation of number.   Number was in danger of loosing its complex hierarchical structure and its potency as a theological symbol.

Is it proper to call Pythagorean and Neo-Platonic speculation 'mathematics' at all?   Would it not be better to say simply that a small amount of real mathematics happened to be worked out rather fortuitously under the auspices of alien speculative and religious motives?   Surely Stevin was a representative of real mathematics whereas his opponents were anti-mathematical.   They did not represent an alternative way of doing mathematics, but rather a way of not doing mathematics at all. As Stark (1958) has argued in a similar context: 'If we may so express it, their mathematics was like ours, but it was overlaid with magic' (p. 162).

What this response shows is that our thinking about mathematics is poised on a knife-edge. By adopting a formal, either/or attitude it can be made to look as if there are no significant sources of variation within mathematics which require explanation. Clearly if we do not recognise number mysticism as a form of mathematics at all then there is no question of it being an alternative. If we allow ourselves actively to sort out and divide historical examples into genuinely mathematical components and those parts which are not deemed mathematics at all then the eternal, self-sufficient unity of mathematics will be guaranteed. It will be guaranteed because it will be an artefact of our evaluations. It is possible to protest against this formalistic attitude on these grounds: that it makes it tautological that there is no alternative mathematics. It is saying that there is no 'true' alternative mathematics, whilst insisting on the right to define what is to count as 'true'. But examples are better than formal protests. The next example will confront the premise underlying these formal, knife-edge attitudes. This is the assumption that mathematics can be rightly thought of in isolation from a context of interpretive principles which give it meaning. What stands in the way of a sociology of mathematics is the idea that mathematics has a life of its own and a meaning of its own. This is to assume that there is an intrinsic significance which resides in the symbols themselves awaiting to be perceived or understood. Without this assumption there would be no historical justification for factoring out what is to count as proper mathematics. There would be no basis for retrospectively isolating and discriminating 'true' mathematics.

THE METAPHYSICS OF ROOT TWO

Today it is taken for granted that the square root of two is a number: namely the number which, when multiplied by itself yields as a product the number 2. It is usually called an irrational number, which is a name left over from the time when there was considerable concern over its status. The worry lay in the fact, well known to Aristotle, that no fraction p/q could ever precisely equal the square root of 2.

The proof that Aristotle gave of this is based on the following idea. Suppose that root 2 were equal to some fraction p/q. Further, assume that this fraction had been simplified by cancelling any factors which were common to its top and bottom. In particular this means that you cannot still divide both p and q by 2. So we can write:

assume $$\frac{p}{q} = \sqrt{2}$$

therefore $$p^2 = 2q^2$$

This means that p squared must be an even number because it equals a number which has 2 as a factor, namely 2q squared. But if p squared is

even then p must be even.   Now if p is even then q must be odd because
it has been assumed that p/q had been simplified and any common factors
such as 2 removed.   If p is even it can be represented as follows:

$$p = 2n$$

so
$$p^2 = 4n^2 = 2q^2$$

therefore
$$q^2 = 2n^2$$

Now the same sequence of arguments which had established that p is even
and q odd can be carried through for q.   If q squared equals 2n squared
then q squared must be even and so q must be even.   Therefore p must be
odd.   Of course this is the direct opposite to what has just been concluded.
What is more this whole sequence of steps may be mechanically repeated.
The result is that p and q are now assigned to the category of even number,
now to that of odd number, now to even again, and so on.

It is usual to terminate the calculation after the first shift of p from
being even to being odd and to deem this an evident contradiction.   The
existence of this contradiction means that one of the premises of the
argument must be wrong, and the only dubious assumption was that the
square root of 2 can be represented by a fraction like p/q.   So this is
rejected.

What does this sequence of calculations mean and how does it get the
meaning that is assigned to it?   Does the calculation prove that root 2 is
an irrational number?   Strictly it only shows that root 2 is not a rational
number, but to us it can hardly have any other meaning: if root 2 is not a
rational number it is an irrational number.   This is not however what it
proved to the Greeks.   To them it proved that the square root of 2 was
not a number at all.   This series of computations was one of their
reasons for keeping apart all considerations which applied to numbers,
properly so called, from considerations which applied to magnitudes.
Geometrical lengths for example which are of length root 2 can be specified,
e.g. the hypotenuse of a right-angled triangle which has sides of unit
length.   This only shows what a gulf separates geometry from arithmetic.

What, then, does the proof really prove?   Does it prove that the
square root of 2 is not a number or that it is an irrational number?
Clearly what it proves depends on the background assumptions about
number within which the calculation is viewed.   If number basically means
counting number, a collection or pattern of dots, then the calculation will
mean something quite different than if number has been intuitively blended
with the image of the continuous line.

The proof will not have any 'intrinsic' significance.   It will make no
sense to scrutinise its elementary steps in the hope that the meaning of the
proof will reside in the marks on the paper or the symbolic routines of the
computation itself.   This is particularly evident from the fact that these
routines form an unending sequence which can be repeated over and over

again.   There is nothing in the computation itself to stop anyone playing
the game of showing that p and q are even and then odd over and over
again.

We can even imagine that this version of the calculation could prompt
the thought that here was a proof that p and q were both odd and even.
Why would this be an absurdity?   Imagine a culture in which men had
learned many significant things in arithmetic but had never set much store
by the categories of odd and even.   They may have utilised such properties in some of their calculations, but suppose they had never
separated out this divide or attached great importance to it.   They would
not, for instance, in this culture have dreamt of errecting a Table of
Opposites like the Pythagoreans, let alone setting out the odd and the even
in correspondence with other cosmic dichotomies.   Perhaps, unlike the
Pythagoreans, night and day, good and bad, and black and white did not
even seem to be obvious or important opposites.   After all, night shades
into day, good into bad and black into white.   Suppose that we are speaking of a nation of compromisers, mediators, mixers and blenders, whose
world-view and social circumstances emphasise the intermingling of
things.   Such a cosmology would be intelligible and could be highly
sophisticated.   The computation, read as a proof that numbers can be
both odd and even, would fit neatly and naturally, and would further
confirm the belief that rigid boundaries were unrealistic.

The point behind this fanciful example is the same as that behind
the historical case that preceded it.   Certain conditions have to obtain
before a computation has any meaning.   These conditions are social in
the sense that they reside in the collectively held system of classifications
and meanings of a culture.   Consequently they will vary and as they vary
so will the meaning of pieces of mathematics.

If the particular meaning of a computation depends on background
assumptions its general influence is even more contingent.   The discovery
of irrational magnitudes is often called the 'crisis of irrationals' in Greek
mathematics.   It was a crisis because the separation of magnitude and
number that it suggested to the Greeks was opposite to their previous
tendency to imagine lines and shapes as built up out of dots.   (Popper
gives a lively account of this cosmology of number atomism in chapter 2
of his 'Conjectures and Refutations' (1963).)   The discovery may indeed
have brought about the decline of the earlier approach but there is no need
for it to have done so.   What was a crisis need have been no more than an
unfortunate anomaly.   Had those who subscribed to this cosmology found
other expressions of its basic standpoint, other work to do, no crisis need
have ensued.   The contingency of the outcome is clear from the fact that
centuries later the same number atomism again became the basis for
creative work.   For example, the seventeenth-century French
mathematician, Roberval, imagined lines to be made up of dots and proceded to use arithmetical devices like summation and approximation to
find areas of triangles, volumes of pyramids and sums of cubes and
higher powers.   He proved results that we now see as special cases in

the integral calculus (cf. Boyer (1959), p. 142).   Perhaps an early Greek
Roberval would have staved off the crisis of irrationals.   Certainly the
theorem about the square root of two did not inhibit Roberval's work.

A similar case of mathematical procedures which are endowed with
a different significance at different times is provided by the use of
infinitesimals.   This will be the next example.   It also illustrates the
ebb and flow of standards of rigour in mathematics.

INFINITESIMALS

It is sometimes said that 'really' a curve is made up of many little
straight lines.   Clearly the analogy between a smooth curve and a set of
straight lines connected end to end may increase the smaller and more
numerous the segments.   This and similar intuitions were at the root of
the idea of infinitesimals and the notion of 'limits'.   In the limit perhaps
the minute segments of line would actually be identical to the curve (see
Figure 8).   The long history of such ideas culminated in the calculus.

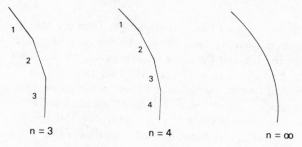

FIGURE 8   Segments and limits

Thinking in terms of infinitesimals also amounts to seeing areas and
solids as if they were made up of segments or slices or elements.   In this
way an intellectual grasp can be achieved of shapes that would otherwise be
difficult to understand.

The history of infinitesimals is very complicated but for the present
argument only a few general points need be illustrated.   In the sixteenth
and seventeenth centuries the use of infinitesimals became very common
in mathematical thinking.   One of the leading exponents was Cavalieri
(1598-1647).   He explicitly invoked analogies between the way a solid was
built out of infinitesimal segments and the way the bulk of a book is made
up out of the thin   sheets of its pages.   He also suggested that a surface
is constructed out of infinitesimal lines in the same way that a cloth is
made up out of thin threads (Boyer (1959), p. 122).

A typically bold use of infinitesimals around the same time is in
Wallis's (1616-1703) derivation of the formula for the area of a triangle.
Think of a triangle made up of tiny parallelograms whose thickness is, as
Wallis put it, 'scarcely anything but a line' (Boyer (1959), p. 171).   The

area of each parallelogram is very nearly equal to its base times its height.   If we assume with Wallis that there is actually an infinity (∞) of such segments then the height of each segment is h/∞, where h is the overall height of the triangle.   The total area is clearly the sum of the areas of the parallelograms.   The first at the vertex will be zero, a mere point.   The last segment will have an area b (h/∞) where b is the length of the base and h/∞ is its infinitesimal height, (see Figure 9).

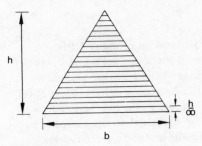

FIGURE 9

Starting from the top, each segment will be a little longer than the last by the addition of a small constant quantity each time.   So the lengths of all the parallelograms between the top and the base will form an arithmetical progression.   Wallis knew that the sum of the terms of an arithmetical progression was the number of terms multiplied by their average value. He saw no reason why this model or pattern of inference should not be applied to his infinite sequence of infinitesimal segments.   So the area of the triangle was obtained by multiplying the following quantities: the average length of a segment b/2; the number of segments, which was infinite ∞; the height of each segment h/∞.   Hence:

$$\text{Total area} = \frac{b}{2} \cdot \infty \cdot \frac{h}{\infty}$$

cancelling the infinite quantities yields:

$$\text{Total area} = \tfrac{1}{2} \text{ base . height.}$$

Many other ingeneous lines of thought of a similar kind produced a burst of investigations and results.   The precise status of infinitesimals was by no means agreed upon but work went ahead.   Why for example isn't Wallis' symbol $1/\infty$ equal to zero?   How can a summation of zero-sized elements yield the finite area of the triangle?   Some thinkers such as Cavalieri were agnostic about the reality of infinitesimals.   Others like Galileo produced lengthy philosophical arguments in their favour (cf. Carruccio (1964), p.200).

Historians looking back on this fruitful period sometimes remark on the lack of rigour attending the use of infinitesimals.   Certainly for modern mathematicians the terms of Wallis' calculation do not have any strict meaning.   Currently, no sense or use can be found for symbols like ∞/∞ or for the operation of cancelling out infinities.   On the other hand historians have certainly acknowledged the value of the decline in rigour which allowed these terms for the first time to feature explicitly in calculations.   Before this time they were forbidden, and they are for-bidden now.   As the historian Boyer says, 'luckily' men like Wallis did not worry too much about rigour (1959, p.169).

Long before Wallis' time the Greek thinker Archimedes had also seen the utility of imagining that shapes could be sliced up.   Archimedes had used this idea along with even more mechanically based metaphors to facilitate a mathematical grasp of some difficult shapes and figures.   For example he imagined how segments of different shaped figures may be balanced against one another.   In this way he was able to set up equations which yielded the volume of the sphere by relating it to simpler shapes like the disc and the cone (see Polya (1954), vol. I, p.155, section 5, for a description of this reasoning).

This 'Method of Mechanical Theorems' is outlined by Archimedes in a letter where he points out that it does not really prove or demonstrate the theorems it suggests (Carruccio (1964)): 'In fact I myself saw some things for the first time through mechanical means, and then I demon-strated them geometrically; because the research done in this way is not real demonstration' (p.111).

A real proof for Archimedes is a geometrical one, not one based on mechanical metaphors of slicing and balancing.   These geometrical proofs conformed to the requirement that no actual infinities were involved. The decline in rigour in the sixteenth century was precisely the growing conviction that the style which Archimedes saw as merely heuristic really did prove things.   Interestingly the later mathematicians did not know about the method that Archimedes had used to find his results.   They only knew the geometrical version into which the proof had been cast.   This gave no clues to the underlying thoughts and motives behind the reasoning. The opinion was therefore common that Archimedes must have had a secret method for doing his mathematics - and indeed he had.   The secret, however, was an historical accident: Archimedes' account of his method was not rediscovered until 1906.

The great trend towards rigour in nineteenth century mathematics reimposed the ban on actual infinities and infinitesimals which had been present many centuries earlier in Greek thought but which had lapsed in the sixteenth century.   The new rigour reconstructed the achievements of men like Cavalieri and Wallis which had culminated in the calculus.   This reconstruction ruled out many of the methods through which those achieve-ments had been won.   Wallis's multiplication by $1/\infty$ and his confident cancellation of infinities from the numerator and denominator of fractions was seen no more.

This oscillation suggests that there may be two different factors or processes in mathematics which are in a state of tension with one another or, at least, which may be mixed in varying proportions.   Underlying the mathematics which we now associate with the calculus there has been a constant intuition that smooth curves, shapes or solids can be seen as being really segmented.   This is a model or metaphor which has frequently appealed to men when they have sought to think about such topics.   Of course mathematics is not the same as intuitive thought.   It is disciplined and controlled.   Imposing themselves on the constant factor have been the varying standards of proof and logical discipline which have been felt appropriate at different times.   For Archimedes the basic, mechanical intuitions had to be filtered through geometry.   This was the only channel of expression that was felt to constitute proper logical control.   The filter was less rigid during the sixteenth century. The intuition could express itself with a fuller, metaphorical vigour.   Of course this carried with it the penalty of confusion and divergence of opinion.   There was a greater role for personal belief and creative variation but this carried the threat of a breakdown of certainty with the unchecked proliferation of disagreement, anomaly and idiosyncrasy.

An important problem follows from seeing variations of rigour in this way.   What factors determine the historical balance between the common, intuitive propensities and the varying standards and styles of rigorous control imposed upon them?   The question is not merely one of the amount of rigorous control but also its particular form.

This problem is identical to that at present being vigorously tackled by historians of the empirical sciences.   The basic routines of computation and manipulation and the basic intuition of similarities, models and metaphors might be considered to be the empirical or ex-periential aspects of mathematics.   It would correspond to the input of data from experience and experiment in the natural sciences.   The higher interpretive principles which embody meaning, proof and rigour correspond to the explanatory theories, paradigms, research programmes and metaphysical frameworks of the natural scientist.   There appears to be no reason why mathematics should be treated any differently to the empirical sciences.   More will be said about this below.

CONCLUSION

A number of cases have now been presented which can be read as examples of alternative forms of mathematical thought to our own.   By exhibiting divergences of style, meaning, association and standards of cogency they make it clear that there are significant variations in mathematical thought which need explaining.   Further, it is plausible to suppose that these variations may be illuminated by looking for social causes.

The examples also provided evidence to reinforce the (modified) form of Mill's theory.   They have shown mathematics to be grounded in experience but experience which is selected according to varying principles and endowed with varying meaning, connections and uses.   In particular the examples have also reinforced the idea that one part of experience is used as a model with which to view a wide range of problems. Analogical and metaphorical extension of these models has featured prominently.

These variations in mathematical thought are often rendered invisible.   One tactic for achieving this end has already been remarked upon.   This is the knife-edge insistence that a style of thinking only deserves to be called mathematics in as far as it approximates to our own. There are however other ways of disguising variation which are less obvious.   These are frequently represented in the writing of the history of mathematics.

Writing history is necessarily an interpretive process.   What mathematicians in the past have thought and concluded has to be given some contemporary meaning or gloss if it is to be intelligible.   There are many ways of doing this: comparing and contrasting; sorting the valuable from the valueless; separating the meaningful from the meaningless; trying to discover system and coherence; interpreting the obscure and incoherent; filling in gaps and drawing attention to errors; explaining what a thinker might, could, or would have done given more information, insight and luck than he actually had; providing detailed commentary which reconstructs underlying assumptions and guiding beliefs; and so on.   This apparatus of scholarly commentary and interpretation unavoidably mediates our grasp of the past.   It is a formidable and extensive apparatus.   In due proportion to its size is its scope for imposing the standards and preoccupations of the present on to the past.   Indeed some such imposition is a necessary feature of all understanding.   The only question is: what standards shall be imposed and what concerns will govern the work which is put into the manufacture of our sense of the past?

If an historian should desire to show the cumulative character of mathematics then his interpretive apparatus will enable him to do so. Counter examples to his vision of progress will become periods of slow development or deviation into error or wrong turnings.   Instead of alternatives being exhibited the task becomes one of sorting out the wheat from the chaff.   No wonder that it was possible for the historian Cajori (1919), writing at the same time as Spengler, to say that mathematics is preeminently a cumulative science; that nothing is lost; and that the contributions of the distant past shine as brightly today as do modern contributions.

It would be unjust and too simple to say that in such accounts history had been falsified.   No standards of integrity or scholarly industry are violated.   Indeed such virtues are impressively and abundantly evident. Rather it should be said that these virtues are all employed in the interests of an overall progressivist vision, and it is this which must be challenged. The examples in this chapter have born out the prediction of the naturalistic approach: there is discontinuity and variation within mathematics as well as discontinuity between mathematics and what is not mathematics.   Other values must move us if these are to be brought to light fully and seen as problems demanding explanation.   One such value, for example, is a concern for the mechanics of logical and mathematical thought.   This issue was obviously involved in the discussion of Frege and Mill, and it will be my concern in the next chapter.

Chapter 7

NEGOTIATION IN LOGICAL AND MATHEMATICAL THOUGHT

It is the purpose of this chapter to take up again the analysis of logical compulsion. The intention is to add to the account given so far an entirely new process, which I shall call 'negotiation'. The claim of chapter 5 was that the compelling character of our reasoning is a form of social compulsion. This is too simple as it stands because social conventions, norms, or institutions do not, and cannot, always compel by the direct internalisation of a sense of right and wrong. Just as men haggle over questions of duty and legality so they haggle over questions of logical compulsion. Just as our roles and obligations may conflict so may the deliverances of our logical intuitions. These unavoidable and cross-cutting demands find no explanation or resolution in the account given so far. When these factors have been taken into account a richer picture will emerge of the creative or generative powers of thought. A more sophisticated understanding will be possible of just what the compulsion of a logical or mathematical argument amounts to. It will be a picture which, more than ever, demands a sociological perspective to do it justice.

One approach to these issues is to return to Mill's 'Logic'. In the course of a rather dry disagreement that Mill was having with Bishop Whately he dropped some disturbing and exciting hints about the nature of formal reasoning. The context is unpromising. Mill is debating with Whately the question: does the syllogism contain a 'petitio principii'? The issue can be stated very simply by looking at the following syllogistic argument:

All men are mortal
The Duke of Wellington is a man
Therefore the Duke of Wellington is mortal

If we are in a position to assert the first premise, that all men are mortal, then we must already know that the Duke is mortal. So what are we doing when we conclude or infer his mortality at the end of the syllogism? Surely the syllogism begs the question or reasons in a circle? Mill believes that there is indeed a circle here. Part of the subsequent account of reasoning that he gives to justify this view is well known, but some of its most suggestive features pass unnoticed.

LORD MANSFIELD'S ADVICE

The familiar part of Mill's theory is that reasoning proceeds, as he puts it, from particulars to particulars.   Bearing in mind that the Duke of Wellington was alive when Mill wrote, then the inference to his mortality was by inductive generalisation and the association of ideas.   Experience yields reliable inductive generalisations concerning death and these are naturally extrapolated to cover cases which appear relevantly similar to those occurring in the past.   The case of the Iron Duke is assimilated to the previous cases signalised by the generalisation.   Mill says that the real process of inferring consists in the move from particular past cases to particular new cases.   The thought process involved does not therefore really depend on, or proceed via, the generalisation that all men are mortal.   It gets along without the help of the major premise of the syllogism.   As Mill put it: 'Not only may we reason from particulars to particulars without passing through generals, but we perpetually do so reason' (II, III, 3).
        If the general premise of a syllogism is not involved in our acts of reasoning then what status is to be assigned to it?   This is where Mill drops his hints.   General propositions for Mill are merely 'registers' of inferences that we have already made.   The reasoning, he insists, lies in the specific acts of assimilating the new cases to the old ones, 'not in interpreting the record of that act'.   In the same discussion Mill refers to the generalisation that all men are mortal as a 'memorandum'.   The inference to the mortality of any specific person does not, says Mill, follow from the memorandum itself but rather from those very same past cases which were themselves the basis of the memorandum.
        Why call the major premise of a syllogism a record, a register or a memorandum?   To talk of premises and principles in this way conveys two ideas.   First, it suggests that they are derivative or mere epi-phenomena.   Second, whilst indicating that they are not central to the act of reasoning itself, it hints that they do perform some other positive function, albeit not the one that is usually attributed to them.   Mill's language here suggests a book-keeping or bureaucratic role, a means of documenting and filing what has happened.
        Mill neatly epitomises and extends this account by his story of Lord Mansfield's advice to a judge.   This was to give decisions boldly because they would probably be right, but on no account to give reasons for them, for these would almost infallibly be wrong.   Lord Mansfield knew, says Mill, that the assigning of reasons would be an afterthought.   The judge in fact would be guided by his past experience, and it would be absurd to suppose that the bad reason would be the source of the good decisions.
        If reasons do not produce conclusions, but are mere afterthoughts,

then what relation do they bear to them?   Mill sees the connection between general principles and the cases that fall under them as something which has to be created.   An interpretive bridge has to be built. Thus: 'This is a question, as the Germans express it, of hermeneutics. The operation is not a process of inference, but a process of interpretation' (II, III, 4).

Mill treats the syllogism in a similar way.   Its formal structures are connected to actual inferences by an interpretive process.   It is 'a mode in which our reasonings may always be represented'.   That is to say: formal logic represents a mode of display; an imposed discipline; a contrived and more or less artificial surface structure.   This display must itself be the product of a special intellectual effort and must itself involve some form of reasoning.   What is striking is the order of causality and priority that this account reveals.   The central idea is that formal principles of reason are the tools of informal principles of reasoning. Deductive logic is the creature of our inductive propensities;   it is the product of interpretive afterthoughts.   I shall refer to this idea as the priority of the informal over the formal.

How does the priority of the informal over the formal express itself? The answer is two-fold.   First, informal thought may use formal thought. It may seek to strengthen and justify its predetermined conclusions by casting them in a deductive mould.   Second, informal thought may seek to criticise, evade, outwit or circumvent formal principles.   In other words the application of formal principles is always a potential subject for informal negotiation.   This negotiation is what Mill referred to as an interpretive or hermeneutic process.   It concerns the link which must always be forged between any rule and any case which allegedly falls under that rule.

The relation between the formal principles or logic and informal reasoning is clearly a delicate one.   Informal thought seems at one and the same time to acknowledge the existence and the potency of formal thought - why else would it exploit it? - and yet it has a will of its own. If Mill is right it goes its own way, moving inductively from particular to particular, governed by associative links.   How can it do both of these things at once?

Consider the syllogism: all A is B, C is an A, therefore C is B. This is a compelling pattern of reasoning.   It emerges out of our learning of simple properties of physical containment.   We have an informal tendency to reason as follows: if a coin is put in a matchbox and the matchbox is put in a cigar box, then we go to the cigar box to retrieve the coin. This is the prototype of the syllogism.   The simple situation provides a model for the general pattern which comes to be counted as formal, logical and necessary.   Formal principles, like the syllogism above, thus harness a natural proclivity to draw conclusions.   For this reason it can represent a valuable ally or an important enemy in any case that is being made.   It may therefore become important to subsume a problematic case under this pattern or to keep them apart, depending on the informal purposes.

In order to evade the force of an inference it is obviously necessary to challenge the application of the premises, or the concepts in the premises, to the case in hand. Perhaps the item designated by the letter C is not really an A; perhaps not all things counted as As really are Bs. In general, distinctions must be drawn; boundaries re-allocated; similarities and differences indicated and exploited; new interpretations developed, and so forth. This form of negotiation does not call the syllogistic rule itself into question. After all, the rule is embedded in our experience of the physical world, so some range of application will have to be granted it; and tomorrow we may want to appeal to it ourselves. What can be negotiated is any particular application.

Informal thinking therefore has a positive use for formal principles as well as a need to circumvent them. Whilst some informal purposes will be exerting pressure to modify or elaborate logical structures and meanings, others will be banking on their stability and maintenance. Informal thinking is both conservative and innovatory.

The idea that logical authority is moral authority may be in danger of neglecting these more dynamic elements in logical thought: competing definitions; opposing pressures; contested patterns of inference; problematic cases. To forget these would be to assume that logical authority always works by being taken for granted. The present point is that it also works by being taken into account: by being a component in our informal calculations. Authority which is sustained by being taken for granted may be said to be in static equilibrium to contrast it with the image of dynamic equilibrium. This static acceptance may be a more stable and compelling form of authority but even this stability can be disturbed.

There is no reason why a sociological theory should not allow for both phenomena. Indeed the coexistence of these alternative styles of constraint is a central feature of all aspects of social behaviour. In some people and in some circumstances moral or legal precepts, for example, may be internalised as emotionally charged values which control behaviour. In other cases these precepts may be apprehended simply as pieces of information: things to be born in mind when planning behaviour and predicting the responses of others. The concurrence of these two modes of social influence in mathematics - and the theoretical problem of untangling them - can only serve to strengthen its similarity with other aspects of behaviour.

The negotiated application of formal principles of inference explains certain important examples of variation in logical or mathematical behaviour. Of course, the more formalised the logical principles at issue the more explicit and conscious is the negotiation process; the less explicit the principle, the more tacit the negotiation. I shall illustrate the negotiated character of logical principles with three examples. The first will concern the negotiated overthrow of a self-evident logical truth. The second example concerns the much discussed question of whether the Azande tribesmen have a different logic to us. The third case will be the negotiation of a proof in mathematics. This will be based on the brilliant

historical study of Euler's theorem made by I. Lakatos (1963-4).   Here
Lakatos offers something of great value to the sociologist, much more than
might be guessed from his methodological remarks that I discussed earlier.

PARADOXES OF THE INFINITE

Consider again the syllogism: all As are B, C is an A, therefore C is a B.
It was argued that this reasoning is based on the experience of containment
and enclosure.   If anyone is in doubt as to how or why the syllogism is
correct he need only look at the diagrammatical form into which it can be
cast, and which is equivalent to it (see Figure 10).   The diagram connects
the syllogism to an important common sense principle, namely that the
whole is greater than the part.

FIGURE 10   The whole is greater than the part

It is tempting to assume that because experiences of enclosure are
ubiquitous they will uniformly and without exception impress this principle
on all minds.   It is not surprising that those who believe in the univers-
ality of logic cite such principles in evidence.   Thus Stark (1958) says:
> So far as purely formal propositions are concerned, there simply is
> no problem of relativity.   An example of such a proposition is the
> assertion that the whole is greater than the part.   In spite of all
> that the super-relativists have argued, there can be no society in
> which this sentence would not hold good, because its truth springs
> immediately from the definition of its terms and hence is absolutely
> independent of any concrete extra-mental conditioning (p. 163).

Stark is not saying that this truth is innate.   He allows that it comes from
experience, but so direct is the connection with experience that nothing can
insinuate itself between the mind and its immediate apprehension of this
necessity.   Experiences of this kind are universal and so the self-same
judgments arise. Always and everywhere the whole is greater than the
part.

It is certainly correct to say that this idea is available in all cultures.
It is a feature of our experience which can always be appealed to, and so
some application will always be found.   But this does not mean that any
particular application is compelling or that its truth is immediate, or that
there is no problem of relativity.   Indeed this case is particularly interesting because it shows the opposite of what Stark thinks.   There is a body of

mathematics called transfinite arithmetic which is successfully based on
an explicit rejection of the principle that the whole is greater than the
part. Properly understood this example therefore shows that apparently
self-evident truths backed by compelling physical models can be subverted
and renegotiated.

Consider the sequence of integers: 1, 2, 3, 4, 5, 6, 7, ...
Select from this endless sequence another endless sequence consisting of
only the even numbers, 2, 4, 6, and so on. It is possible to associate
these two sequences thus:

$$1 \quad 2 \quad 3 \quad 4 \quad 5 \quad 6 \quad 7 \quad ...$$

$$2 \quad 4 \quad 6 \quad 8 \quad 10 \quad 12 \quad 14 \quad ...$$

In common sense terms the even numbers can be counted. More technic-
ally it can be said that the even numbers are put in a one-one correspondence with the integers. This one-one correspondence will never
break down. For every integer there will always be a unique even number
to pair with it. Likewise for every even number there will be a unique
integer. Suppose it is now said that sets of objects which have a one-one
correspondence between their members have the same number of members.
This seems intuitively reasonable, but means that there are the same
number of even numbers as there are integers. The even numbers, however, are a selection, a mere part, a subset of all the integers. Therefore the part is as great as the whole and the whole is not greater than the
part.

The inexhaustible supply of integers can be expressed by saying
that there is an infinite number of them. Infinite aggregates thus have
the property that a part can be put in one-one correlation with the whole.
This property of infinite aggregates was known many years before the
development of transfinite arithmetic. It was taken as evidence that the
very idea of aggregates of an infinite size was paradoxical, self-contra-
dictory and logically defective. Cauchy for example denied their
existence on this basis (Boyer (1959), p. 296). However, what had once
been grounds for dismissing infinite sets came to be accepted as their
very definition. Thus Dedekind (1901, p.63) says: 'A system S is said to
be infinite when it is similar to a proper part of itself', where 'similar' in
this definition is what has been called one-one correspondence.

How can a contradiction be transmuted into a definition, how is such
a renegotiation possible? What has happened is that the model of physical
enclosure which underlay the conviction that wholes are greater than their
parts has given away to another dominant image or model: that of objects
being placed in one-one correspondence with each other. This, too, is a
situation which it is easy to exemplify and experience in a direct and concrete way. Once this alternative model has become the centre of attention
then the simple routine of aligning even numbers with integers becomes a

natural basis for concluding that the part (the even numbers) are as great as the whole (all of the integers). Informal thought has subverted an apparently compelling principle by pressing the claims of a new, informal model. A new range of experience has been located and exploited. If compelling logical principles consist in a socially sanctioned selection from our experience then they can always be opposed by appealing to other features of that experience. Formal principles only feel special and privileged because of selective attention. Given new concerns and purposes and new preoccupations and ambitions then the conditions exist for a readjustment.

The conclusion is that there is no absolute sense in which anyone must accept the principle that the whole is greater than the part. The very meanings of the words do not compel any given conclusion because they cannot compel the decision that any new case must be assimilated to the old cases of this rule. At most prior applications of this model creates a presumption that new and similar cases will also fall under the same rule. But presumption is not compulsion, and judgments of similarity are inductive not deductive processes. If it is proper to speak of compulsion then the compelling character of a rule resides merely in the habit or tradition that some models be used rather than others. If we are compelled in logic it will be in the same way that we are compelled to accept certain behaviour as right and certain behaviour as wrong. It will be because we take a form of life for granted. Wittgenstein expressed it neatly when he said in the 'Remarks' (1956): 'Isn't it like this: so long as one thinks it can't be otherwise, one draws logical conclusions.' (I, 155). Nevertheless Wittgenstein believes it is right to say that we are compelled by the laws of inference: in the same way as we are compelled by any other laws in human society. Let us therefore look at a society with very different laws to ours and see if its members are indeed compelled to reason differently.

AZANDE LOGIC AND WESTERN SCIENCE

Evans-Pritchard's (1937) book on the Azande describes a society which is profoundly different from ours. Its most striking feature is that nothing of importance is ever done by a Zande without consulting an oracle. A small quantity of poison is administered to a chicken and a question is put to the oracle in such a way that it can be answered 'yes' or 'no'. The death or survival of the bird conveys the oracle's answer. Every human calamity appears to the Azande to be due to witchcraft. Witches are people whose ill-will and malevolent powers are the cause of trouble. Their main form of detection is, of course, the oracle.

Being a witch is not simply a matter of disposition. It is an inherited physical trait, consisting of a substance in the belly called witchcraft-substance. A male witch will transmit witchcraft-substance to all his sons and a female witch to all her daughters. This substance

can be detected in post-mortem examinations and these are sometimes
undertaken to establish or refute witchcraft accusations.

It would seem a clear logical inference that only one, single, decisive
and incontestable case of witchcraft is needed to establish that a whole line
of people have been or will be witches. Equally a decision that a man is
not a witch should clear all his kinsmen. The Azande, however, do not
act in accordance with these inferences. As Evans-Pritchard puts it:

> To our minds it appears evident that if a man is proven a witch the
> whole of his clan are ipso-facto witches, since the Zande clan is a
> group of persons related biologically to one another through the male
> line. Azande see the sense of this argument but they do not accept
> its conclusions, and it would involve the whole notion of witchcraft
> in contradiction were they to do so (p. 24).

In theory the whole of a witch's clan should be witches. In practice only
close paternal kinsmen of a known witch are also considered witches. Why
is this?

Evans-Pritchard's account is clear and straightforward. He
explains what is happening by considering the degree to which the Azande
give priority to specific and concrete instances of witchcraft rather than to
general and abstract principles. He illustrates their localised focus of
interest by pointing out that the Azande never ask an oracle the general
question of whether such and such a person is a witch. They ask whether
such and such a person is bewitching anyone here and now. Thus:
'Azande do not perceive the contradiction as we perceive it because they
have no theoretical interest in the subject, and those situations in which
they express their beliefs in witchcraft do not force the problem upon them'
(p. 25).

This analysis clearly involves two central ideas. First, there really
is a contradiction in the Azande views whether the Azande see it or not.
The Azande have institutionalised a logical mistake, or at least a degree of
logical blindness. Second, if the Azande were to see the error then one of
their major social institutions would be untenable. It would be under the
threat of being found contradictory or logically defective, and hence its
survival would be endangered. In other words it is vital that the Azande
maintain their logical error on pain of social upheaval and the need for a
radical change in their ways. The first idea is a belief in the uniqueness
of logic; the second idea is a belief in the potency of logic. Logic is
potent because logical confusion may cause social confusion.

Wittgenstein's ideas may be appealed to in order to challenge this
analysis. As the quotation at the end of the last section showed
Wittgenstein sometimes equated the drawing of a logical conclusion with
thinking that something cannot be otherwise. Logical steps are those that
we just take for granted. Now the Azande clearly take it for granted that
the whole of a witch's clan cannot be witches. For them this cannot be
otherwise. On this view it is therefore logical not to draw this conclusion.
But since it is the logical one for us to draw there must be more than one
logic: an Azande logic and a Western logic. The premise of uniqueness
used by Evans-Pritchard is thus rejected.

This approach has been developed by Peter Winch in a paper called Understanding a Primitive Society, (1964).   He argues by quoting from Wittgenstein's 'Remarks'.   We are asked to consider a game: 'such that whoever begins can always win by a particular simple trick.   But this has not been realised - so it is a game.   Now someone draws our attention to it - and it stops being a game' (II, 77).   Notice that it stops being a game rather than that it never was a game.   We are invited to see the game, the state of knowledge of the players, and their consequent attitudes, as all forming a whole.   The game, with the additional knowledge of the trick, constitutes a different whole.   It forms a different game.   Similarly, we should see the Azande beliefs, with their particular boundaries and applications and contexts, as forming a unique, self-sufficient whole. They constitute a particular game that may be played.   Our perception of that whole will be distorted if we see it as a mere fragment of a wider, or different, game.

In order to stress the self-sufficient character of the Azande procedures Winch then draws attention to some differences between the game analogy and the case under discussion.   The old game is indeed rendered obsolete by the new information.   Once the trick is known the old game naturally breaks down under the impact of the knowledge.   This shows that it is not self-contained but is really a precarious part of a wider system.   But the Azande do not simply give up witchcraft when (what we count as) its full logical implications are drawn to their attention.   They are not thrown into confusion.   This, Winch suggests, is evidence that Azande witchcraft and its logic are not comparable to the Western perspective.   They are not related as part to whole.   Theirs is a quite different game that does not have a natural extension into our game.

The important thing to notice about these objections to Evans-Pritchard's analysis is that one and only one of its two central ideas have been challenged.   Winch's case takes issue with the uniqueness of logic; It does not dispute its potency.   Indeed it seems to share this belief.   The criticism appears to grant that if there had been a logical contradiction in Azande beliefs then the institution of witchcraft would indeed have been threatened.   It explains why it is not under any threat by suggesting that there must be a different logic.

If Mill is right then logic is the very opposite of potent.   The application of logical schemata is merely a way of arranging our afterthoughts, and is always a matter for negotiation.   Let us see how the Azande case may be analysed when once this assumption of potency, common to the two previous accounts, has been discarded.

Lord Mansfield would have been proud of the Azande.   They put his advice into action by giving their decisions boldly whilst dispensing with an elaborate structure of justification.   They follow their oracle's pronouncements about who is engaged in witchcraft and with equal confidence they know that not everyone in the malefactors clan is a witch.   These two beliefs are stable and central to their lives.   What then of the logical inference that threatens the whole clan?   The answer is that it is no threat

at all.   There is no danger of their stable beliefs being called into
question.   If the inference ever became an issue the threat would be
deftly negotiated away, and this would not in itself be difficult.   All that
is needed is that a few cunning distinctions be drawn.   For example, it
might be admitted that everyone in the clan had indeed inherited witchcraft-substance but it could be insisted that this did not mean they were
witches.   Really, it might be claimed, everyone in every clan had the
potential to be a witch, but this potential was only actualised in some
people, and these were the only witches properly so called.   There is
evidence that the Azande do sometimes make such moves.   A person who
has once been accused of being a witch will not always be treated as one.
The Azande say that this is because his witchcraft-substance is 'cool'.
For all intents and purposes he is no longer a witch.   Logic poses no
threat to the institution of witchcraft, for one piece of logic can always be
met by another.   Not even this is necessary unless someone uses the
inference in order to pose a threat, and if they do, it is the user not the
logic that is the threat.
      The situation can be represented in the form of Figure 11.

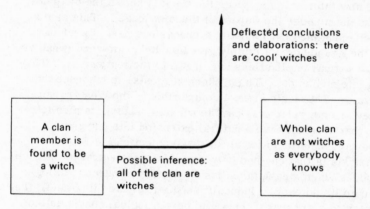

FIGURE 11   The impotence of logic

This shows that the really weighty factors are the two, socially taken-for-
granted elements in the situation: the use of the oracle and the general
innocence of the clan as a whole.   These are sanctioned by tradition and
are central to the Azande form of life.   No mere logical extrapolation
from the one is going to disturb the other.   If any justification for the
coexistance of these two features of society is needed then an appropriate
structure of afterthoughts can be generated.   If one structure of justification fails another can always be produced.
      The fact that we can imagine extending the witchcraft accusation to
the whole of a clan is simply because we do not really feel the pressure
against this conclusion.   We can let our thoughts extend themselves
irresponsibly and unopposed.   If we did feel the pressure of its obvious
absurdity and at the same time felt the need to give reasons we could
easily do so.

The major social variables in this picture obviously fall into two classes.   There are the institutions which are taken for granted and there is the degree of elaboration and development of the ideas which link these institutions together.   In the Azande case the elaboration is minimal. In other cultures it may be highly developed.   The extent and direction of this elaboration may be plausibly assumed to be a function of men's social purposes and the style and intensity of their interactions.   It would not be something that would grow or fail to grow for no reason, as if it were a spontaneous efflorescence, or something governed by its own inner dialectic.   It will grow as far as the situation causes it to grow, and no further.

To see the justice of this conclusion consider an example.   Suppose that an alien anthropologist reasoned with us as follows: in your culture a murderer is someone who deliberately kills someone else.   Bomber pilots deliberately kill people.   Therefore they are murderers.   We can see the point of this inference but would no doubt resist the conclusion. Our grounds would be that the alien observer did not really understand what a murderer was.   He could not see the difference between the two cases that he had conflated.   Perhaps we would reply: murder is an act of individual volition.   Bomber pilots are performing a duty, and this duty is specifically sanctioned by governments.   We distinguish the special roles appropriate to the armed forces.   Consulting his notebook the anthropologist might then tell us that he has seen men shaking their fists at attacking aeroplanes and shouting murderer after them.   Our reply to this could then be that there is indeed an analogy between murder and killing in war, and it was no doubt the similarities rather than the differences that were uppermost in the mind of the victims whom he had observed.   We may add that it is hardly to be expected that men will be completely logical under such provocation and that what was observed was an understandable lapse from the canons of strictly rational conduct.   The anthropologist might then ply us with more questions about (civilian) car-drivers who kill people.   No doubt he would be fascinated by the intricate way in which the concepts of accident, manslaughter, chance, responsibility, mistake and intention have proliferated in our culture.   The anthropologist might even conclude that we see the point of his arguments but attempt to evade their logical force by an 'ad hoc' and shifting tangle of metaphysical distinctions.   In that culture, he would perhaps say, they have no practical interest in logical conclusions.   They prefer their metaphysical jungle because otherwise their whole institution of punishment would be threatened.

The sceptical anthropologist would be wrong.   We do not reason like this in order to protect our institutions from collapse under the pressure of logical criticism.   Rather, it is because we routinely accept the activities of bomber pilots and car-drivers that we adjust our reasoning. The institutions are stable and our informal reasoning makes the necessary adjustments.   In as far as we may feel the force of the anthropologist's logical inferences it is because we are already critical of the institutions.

Being critical means being seized of the analogy between murder and the other activities.   The informal inductive assimilation of the cases is prior to the formal steps in which we could logically display our condemnation.

This process of elaboration is a general feature of our culture and pervades our science quite as much as it does our common sense.   An interesting example of this from the history of science again concerns the much despised phlogiston theory of combustion.   On this theory, it will be recalled, what we now call an oxide was thought, to begin with, to be a simple substance which was called a 'calx'.   The theory proceded on the assumption that:

$$METAL = CALX + PHLOGISTON$$

When a metal was burned, and turned into a calx, then the phlogiston was removed from it.   It was known however that the calx was heavier than the metal.   The removal or extraction of the phlogiston resulted in an increase in weight.   How can something be taken away and yet cause an increase?   It is tempting here to think of the subtraction of a negative number, for this is equivalent to adding, thus: $-(-a) = +a$.   It is therefore easy to believe that the logical conclusion to draw from the experimental result is that phlogiston must have a 'negative weight'.   Historians sometimes say that the phlogiston theory 'implies' that phlogiston has negative weight, (e.g. Conant (1966)).   Obviously negative weight is rather an odd property so this implication is held to show that the theory is odd or implausible or doomed to failure.   In fact most of those who adhered to this theory did not feel compelled to draw this conclusion.   Rather, as good followers of Newton, they felt compelled not to entertain the notion of negative weight.

What they said instead was very simple.   When phlogiston leaves a metal another substance steps in and takes its place.   The extraction of phlogiston does not leave a pure calx but a mixture of calx and something else.   Water was the candidate chosen because it seemed to be implicated in a number of reactions involving phlogiston and its precise role was at that time rather obscure.   The theory was a step towards making it less obscure.   So now, assuming that phlogiston has a genuine and positive weight, its removal can still be accompanied by an increase in weight. All that is required is that the water which steps into its place has a greater weight.   The logical compulsion which follows from a model of simple subtraction is circumvented by a model of replacement.

To those who are determined to see the worst in this venerable old theory such an elaboration will appear to be nothing but a display of perverse ingenuity.   It will be greeted with exasperation, as if it is a mere attempt to evade the true but damning logical conclusion that phlogiston has negative weight.   In reality it is a quite standard move in elaborating a scientific theory.   It was identical to a move made some years later to help the atomic theory of chemistry out of a difficult situation (Nash (1966)).

Gay-Lussac discovered a neat empirical regularity in the way gases combine. Suppose two gases A and B combine to form a gas C. He found that 1 volume of gas A always combined with 1, 2, 3, or some small, whole number of volumes of gas B, provided the volumes are measured under the same conditions of temperature and pressure. Dalton's atomic theory had taught scientists the value of thinking of chemical combinations as taking place by direct combinations of atoms. Gay-Lussac's results thus suggested that if 1 volume of A combined with, say, 1 volume of B, this must be because the same volumes of the gases contained the same number of atoms.

The only trouble with this simple and very useful idea was that sometimes 1 volume of A would combine with 1 volume of B to produce a gas C which would occupy 2 volumes at the same temperature and pressure. This was the case with nitrogen and oxygen. The idea that the volumes contained the same number of atoms could now only be maintained if the atoms split in half. Without this the double volume would only have half the number of atoms per volume. Dalton resisted this conclusion and was prepared to sacrifice the neat experimental result and the useful and simple idea that it suggested. Surely atoms were indivisible; so perhaps Gay-Lussac had oversimplified his experimental findings?

The conclusion that atoms must be split in order to maintain the simple idea that there are the same number in the same volume is, however, easily avoidable. All that has to be assumed is that each particle of gas really consists of two atoms. When A and B combine what then happens is that the compound is formed by 1 atom of A replacing 1 atom of B. Combination takes place, not by means of simple addition, but once again by means of replacement. This was Avagadro's hypothesis. Its physical and chemical plausibility was difficult to establish but its logical basis is very simple. As an elaboration of the basic tenets of atomic theory it is close to that by which the phlogiston theory was developed.

This all suggests that the Azande think very much as we do. Their reluctance to draw the 'logical' conclusion from their beliefs is very similar to our reluctance to abandon our common sense beliefs and our fruitful scientific theories. Indeed their apparent refusal to be logical has the very same basis as does our development of refined and sophisticated theoretical structures. Their beliefs about witchcraft appear to be responsive to the same forces as our beliefs, although of course the forces work to different degrees and in different directions. Our inferences are more often embedded in a set of justificatory distinctions. We keep more elaborate registers and records of our more elaborate negotiations, and our memoranda note different things. Nevertheless the similarities make it plausible to strive for an explanatory theory of intellectual elaboration which covers both the Azande and the atomic scientist.

Where does this leave the question of whether the Azande have a different logic to us? The picture that has emerged is that the Azande

have the same psychology as us but radically different institutions.   If
we relate logic to the psychology of reasoning we shall be inclined to say
that they have the same logic; if we relate logic more closely to the
institutional framework of thought then we shall incline to the view that
the two cultures have different logics.   It would accord with the previous
chapters on mathematics to choose the latter course.   Far more important than such definitional matters however is the basic acknowledgment
that both psychological and institutional factors are involved in reasoning.
Our natural proclivities to infer, like our natural proclivities in all other
directions, do not in themselves form an ordered and stable system.
Some impersonal structure is needed to draw boundaries and to allocate
each tendency to a sphere deemed proper for it.   Because there is no
natural state of equilibrium one line of inference will as surely come into
conflict with another as one appetite or desire will with another.   To give
free-reign, or natural expression, to one tendency only means curtailing
others all the more.   This makes the problem of allocation, and hence
the necessity for negotiation, unavoidable.

Here is a mathematical illustration of this point.   Recall that the
proof that the squared root of 2 is not a rational number contained steps
which could be given free-reign, but which are certainly not allowed their
'natural' expression in contemporary mathematics.   The routine whereby
a number is proved first odd and then even can be repeated over and over
again.   What in fact happens is that this conclusion is brought into collision with the assumption that a number cannot be both odd and even.
The outcome is neither static confrontation, nor the rejection of one side
or the other of the opposition.   Instead a distinction is drawn.   For the
Greeks it was the distinction between numbers and magnitudes; for us it
is the distinction between rational and irrational numbers.

Negotiations create meanings.   The conclusion that the square root
of 2 is an irrational number is not to be discovered within any of the concepts to be involved in the negotiation.   It is thrown up in the situation to
solve a problem and as such it is responsive to the various forces in the
situation.   That is why the Greeks generated a different response to us.
The boundaries and content of our concepts are no more discovered than
are the boundaries of our countries or the content of our institutions.
They are created.   This will now be illustrated with another case from
the history of mathematics.   It shows with great transparency the
generative character of negotiation.

THE NEGOTIATION OF A PROOF IN MATHEMATICS

Around 1752 Euler noticed the following fact: take a solid such as a cube
or a pyramid and count up the number of corners or vertices (V), the
number of edges (E), and the number of faces (F).   It will be found that
they satisfy the formula: $V - E + F = 2$.   A quick check of other figures,
such as those in Figure 12, shows that the formula works for them too.

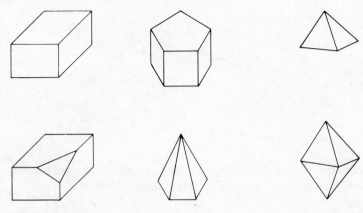

FIGURE 12

Figures of this kind are called polyhedra and the shapes of their surfaces
are polygons.   Euler believed that his formula held true for all polyhedra
and on the basis of checking a large number of cases felt justified in calling the result a theorem.   Nowadays a result arrived at in this way would
never be dignified by the name of a theorem.   It would be held to possess
no more than inductive or moral certainty.   Inductive generalisations may
always fall foul of a subsequent counter example.   A genuine theorem
must have a proof.

The nature of proof and the kind of certainty that it yields is something with which any naturalistic account of mathematics must come to
terms.   The usual picture of a proof is that it endows a theorem with
complete certainty and finality.   This would seem to lift mathematical
theorems beyond the reach of socio-psychological theories.   By using
Lakatos's analysis of the protracted debate over Euler's theorem some
stereotyped ideas about the nature of proof may be broken down and the
way opened for a naturalistic approach.

In 1813 Cauchy proposed an ingenious idea which seemed to prove
Euler's theorem.   It centred around a 'thought-experiment' which can be
performed on polyhedra.   Imagine that the polyhedra were made of sheet
rubber and that one of their faces has been removed.   A count of V, E
and F will now yield a value of F reduced by one.   This means that
$V - E + F = 1$ provided of course that the original formula, equalling 2,
applied to the figure.   Because the figure has had a face removed it is
possible to imagine it opened out and stretched flat.   The cube and the
pentagonal prism, for example, would look like this when stretched out:

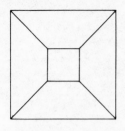
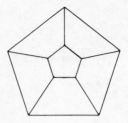

FIGURE   13

The next step in the proof is to draw diagonal lines on the stretched shapes so that the surfaces are turned into sets of triangles.   Thus:

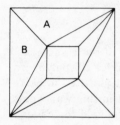

FIGURE 14

By adding an edge to make a triangle the number E is obviously increased by 1, and so is the number F of faces.   Every new edge creates a new face.   The value of the sum V - E + F is therefore unaltered in the tri-angulation process because the two increases cancel one another out in the formula.

The final step in the proof is to remove the triangles one by one. When a triangle, such as that marked A in Figure 14, is removed then one edge and one face disappear.   So still the value of the formula is unaltered. The same applies to a triangle like the one marked B.   Because triangle A has already been removed then the disappearance of B will mean that 2 edges, 1 vertex, and 1 face are taken away.   Again the value of the formula remains unaltered.   Since all of these operations leave the formula unaltered then it can be argued: if Euler's formula held of the original polyhedron then V - E + F = 1 should hold of the one triangle which remains when all the rest have been removed.   It does indeed hold so the original formula is vindicated.

The overall point of the proof is that it shows how the property that Euler noticed is a natural consequence of the fact that a triangle has 3 corners, 3 edges and, of course, 1 face.   The original thought experiment was simply a way of seeing polyhedra as made up of triangles.   This vision was elaborated by clearly displaying and laying out the fact in the stretching and triangulation process.   The work done by the proof con-sists in taking a fact which had emerged from inspection and assimilating it to a better known schema.   Like the model of physical containment, or the model of arranging things in one-one correspondence with one another, the model of stretching and triangulating is an appeal to experience.   It draws attention to elements within our experience, isolates them, and turns them into a routine way of seeing matters.   The puzzling fact is drawn out in terms of the simple schema.

Proofs like Cauchy's obviously violate Lord Mansfield's advice. By giving reasons for their claim they open up a front along which they may be attacked.   There is perhaps no doubting that some polyhedra fit Euler's formula but it is doubtful whether Cauchy's reasoning explains why this has to be so.   For example, can all polyhedra have a face removed and be stretched out in the way that the proof requires; does triangulation always produce one new face for every new edge; does any removal of a triangle leave the formula unchanged?   The answer to all these questions is arguably negative.   Cauchy, Lakatos relates, did not notice that the removal of triangles must proceed very carefully by the removal of boundary triangles if the formula is to remain unchanged as the proof requires.

An interesting situation now arises.   The proof intends and appears to increase the necessity of the result, but at the same time it raises more questions than it started with.   The dialectic between the increasing resources that the ideas of a proof furnish on the one hand, and on the other, the generation of new problems and arguments is illuminated by Lakatos with great skill.

Lhuilier in 1812 and Hessel in 1832 both spotted an exception to Euler's theorem and Cauchy's proof.   Consider Figure 15 which shows two cubes nested inside one another, the inside cube can be thought of as a hollow in the larger, surrounding cube.   A direct check on the number of faces, edges and vertices shows that it does not satisfy the theorem. Nor can Cauchy's thought experiment be carried out.   Removing a face from either cube does not allow the cube to be stretched flat.

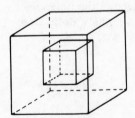

FIGURE 15

When a proof is confronted with a counter example the problem is to decide whether it shows that the proof is not really a proof at all or whether perhaps the counter example is not really a counter example. Perhaps it merely limits the scope of the proof.   If it is assumed that proofs settle once and for all the truth of the proposition proved then something must be wrong with the counter example.   Clearly the counter example of the nested cubes is rather more complicated than the original cases which suggested the theorem, but it certainly satisfies the definition of a polyhedron put forward by Legendre in 1794.   It is, in other words, a solid whose faces are polygons.   Perhaps this definition is wrong and that what should have been meant by a polyhedron, or indeed what perhaps had been intended all along, was that a polyhedron was a surface made up of polygonal faces.   This definition was proposed by Jonquières in 1890. This would rule out the counter example of the nested cubes.   Being a solid, and a peculiar one at that, it no longer needs to be counted as a polyhedron.   The theorem is now safe because it was about polyhedra.

Hessel had an answer to this too.   Consider two pyramids which are joined at a vertex as in Figure 16.   This is a surface made up of polygonal faces but V - E + F = 3 and Cauchy's thought experiment doesn't apply either.   It cannot be stretched flat after the removal of a face.   Of course the same question can be raised: is this oddity a polyhedron?   In 1865 Möbius had already defined a polyhedron in a way which would have barred this counter example.   He said that a polyhedron was a system of polygons such that two polygons meet at every edge and where it is possible to get from one face to another without passing through a vertex.   Clearly the last clause rules out the two pyramids joined at a point.

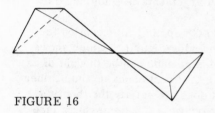

FIGURE 16

Even if Möbius's elaboration of the meaning of polyhedron will rule out Hessel's examples there are still others which slip through the defences. For example the picture frame in Figure 17 satisfies Möbius's definition but Cauchy's proof does not work: it cannot be flattened out.

FIGURE 17

In response to this the proof was narrowed down and stated thus: for simple polyhedra V - E + F = 2, where 'simple' means that they can be flattened out.   Still there are other problems.   A cube with another sitting on top of

FIGURE 18

it produces a snag. The problem this time is not with flattening out but with the process of triangulation, (see Figure 18). When stretched out the shaded area becomes a ring. If a line is added to join A and B during triangulation then the number of edges is increased but not the number of faces. One of the central steps in the proof thus fails. To fend off this problem the theorem can be modified still further. A clause can be added to rule out ring-like faces from the figures to which it applies. Thus it becomes: for simple polyhedra with simply-connected faces $V - E + F = 2$. And so the story proceeds.

The overall process was that the theorem started life as an inductive generalisation. A proof is proposed and this opens out the generalisation to criticism in the very act of showing why it must be true. Counter examples revealed that it was unclear what was and what was not a polyhedron. The meaning of the term 'polyhedron' was in need of decision, for it was quite indeterminate in the shadowy area revealed by the counter examples. It had to be created or negotiated. The proof and the scope of the theorem could then be consolidated by creating an elaborate structure of definitions. These definitions are generated by the collision between the proof and the counter examples. They are the memorandum or register of the course of the negotiations. The proof does not proceed via the definitions. Rather the final, formal structure of the proof is a function of the particular cases that have previously been informally considered. Like Lord Mansfield's afterthoughts Lakatos's definitions really come at the end of a piece of mathematics not at the beginning. Of course the theorem can now be presented as if it proceeded inexorably from the definitions. But these definitions will really reflect the purposes of those who framed them. For example they will reveal what types of figure and what features of figures are held to be important and interesting. The extent of their elaboration will indicate the area where it was necessary to tread carefully, where, for example, adjacent territory had been well worked over for other purposes.

This procedure does not make theorems trivially true or proofs useless. Lakatos reminds us of what Lord Mansfield's advice overlooks: the proof idea is a valuable resource. It is similar to Mill's physical models. It stakes out a claim to understand matters in the light of a certain model and uses it to draw connections and analogies. There are two major ways in which a proof idea functions as a resource. First it allows the anticipation or the creation of counter examples. In the same way that a lawyer scrutinises a case that he has just made out to locate its weak spots and anticipate the likely structure of his opponents arguments so a proof can be scrutinised. Second whether the theorem succeeds or fails the proof idea exists and can be used again as a model and a guide for later work. We have seen how Roberval used the proof ideas of early Greek 'number atomism' even though it had fallen into disrepute after the discovery of irrational magnitudes. Its full resources had been left unexploited.

Lakatos intends his example to show that mathematics like other sciences, proceeds by a method of conjectures and refutations (cf. Lakatos (1962) and (1967)). His efforts to assimilate mathematics to a Popperian epistemology means that he, like the sociologist, wishes to dispel the aura of static perfection and compelling unity that surrounds mathematics. If there is to be a Popperian approach to mathematics then there must be room for criticism, disagreement and change. The more radical the better. Just as in the Popperian analysis of physics and chemistry, there can be no absolute certainty, and no final stopping point when the essence of things stands revealed. Polyhedra have no essence. On this approach there are no ultimate, logical essences in mathematics any more than there are ultimate material essences.

In order to convey this picture Lakatos has concentrated his attention on what he calls 'informal mathematics'. These are the growth areas which have not yet been organised into rigorous deductive systems. To 'formalise' an area of mathematics means presenting its results so that they all flow from a set of explicitly stated axioms. Ideally each step is rendered simple and mechanical so that it proceeds according to explicitly stated rules of inference. For Lakatos this ideal of mathematical knowledge is the death of truly creative thought. The processes of mathematical innovation are obscured by formalisation and the real nature of the knowledge thereby disguised.

The self-evident character that is sometimes claimed for the axioms of formal systems and the intuitively trivial steps of reasoning on which the results are made to depend are, for Lakatos, mere illusions. Something is only obvious because it has not been subject to searching criticisms. Criticism de-trivialises the trivial and shows just how much is always taken for granted in what men find self-evident. There is not, therefore, any ultimate foundation for mathematical knowledge in apparently simple and trivial logical truths.

In rejecting the idea that formalised and axiomatised systems represent the real nature of mathematics Lakatos shows that for him, like Mill, the informal has priority over the formal. This picture of mathematics as conjectural knowledge can find support in the fact that the programme of formalisation and axiomatisation has encountered severe and perhaps insuperable technical problems. These technical difficulties would certainly have been less surprising - and might even have been predictable - had intellectual ideals held sway in mathematics which dispensed with the search for permanent foundations.

To offer a proof of a mathematical result, for Lakatos, is rather like

offering a theoretical explanation for an empirical result in the natural
sciences. Proofs explain why a result, or a conjectural result, is true.
As the discussion of Euler's theorem showed, a proof may be refuted by
counter examples, and saved again by adjusting the scope and content of
definitions and categorisations. Cases which appear to be explained by
a proof may be explained more compellingly in other ways and even turned
into counter-examples as a consequence. Similarly a proof idea which
works, or fails to work, in one area may be put to new and quite different
uses elsewhere, just like the models and metaphors of physical theory.
Like other theories proofs endow what they explain with a meaning. The
invention of new proof ideas or models of inference may radically alter
the meaning of an informal mathematical or logical result. Thus we have
seen that a new interpretation of what it is for two sets to have the same
number of elements allows sense to be attached to the idea that the part
may be as great as the whole. This openness to invention and negotiation,
with all its possibilities for the re-ordering of previous mathematical
activity, means that any formalisation may be subverted. That is: any
rules may be reinterpreted and any ideas may be deployed in new ways.
In principle, informal thought can always outwit formal thought.

The analogy between a proof and an explanation or theory in the
natural sciences provides the opportunity for Lakatos to apply his
Popperian values. The result is easily predictable. Periods of rapid
change in mathematics, when there is active criticism of fundamentals,
are deemed to be good. Periods where definitions, axioms, results and
proofs become taken for granted are counted as periods of stagnation. A
proof which is treated as final and endowed with a rigid certainty becomes
like Newton's theory in physics. This so impressed people that it
numbed their critical faculties. A triumph turned into a disaster.

Almost equally predictable is the connection that Lakatos then makes
between these evaluations and his perception of Kuhn's position. This
link is an important one for the sociologist. Lakatos suggests that periods
of stagnation correspond to periods of 'normal science'. During such
periods certain pieces of mathematics and certain styles of argument
assume the appearance of eternal verities. We have only to look behind
the evaluation (that permanent revolution is good and stability is bad) to
see that this amounts to a sociological theory of logical compulsion. What
is counted as logical is what is taken for granted. At any given time
mathematics proceeds by, and is grounded in, what its practitioners take
for granted. There are no foundations other than social ones.

It is also clear that Lakatos's analysis of mathematics suggests that
something very like a 'Kuhnian' history of mathematics ought to be
possible where taken-for-granted paradigms can be identified in order to
account for the periods of stability or 'stagnation'. In fact contemporary
historians are engaged in writing the history of mathematics in roughly
this way, perhaps participating in the same change of historiographical
style that itself influenced 'The Structure of Scientific Revolutions'. The
rejection of the linear, progressivist assumptions of previous generations
of historians of science is now commonplace.

This newer form of the history of mathematics will deploy exactly the same techniques of scholarship as its predecessor, but it will have different ends in view. It too must synthesise the fragments of incom‑plete documentary evidence and weave a coherent story around the results achieved, the theorems hopefully proved and the disputes that were never fully articulated or resolved. It too needs to interpret, interpolate, comment and expound. But now historians may be more inclined to search for the integrity of different styles of work, to relate things together so that they fall into more or less self-contained epochs, each with their own preoccupations, paradigms or'Weltanschauungen'. Just as before, an underlying unity has to be constructed; the thoughts behind the documents men leave still have to be conjectured.

If the sociology of mathematics simply consisted in such a style of history writing then the historian of mathematics could reasonably insist that he already did the sociology of knowledge. In fact something more, and different, is required for the following reasons. A historiographical style which stresses periodic discontinuity and the integrity of different epochs rather than linear progress can be adopted for many different reasons. Some of these may be quite alien to the perspective of the sociology of knowledge. The fact that Hegelean idealism sees history as made up of epochs with different guiding spirits reminds us that there is no necessary connection here with a causal, scientific approach. More important than the broad patterns and mere style of the history are the problems that it is designed to illuminate. It is the theoretical issues which the researcher illuminates that determines whether the history has any bearing on the sociology of knowledge. This is what gives Kuhn's work its bite.

What problems must the history of mathematics deal with if it is to help the sociology of knowledge? The answer is that it must help to show how and why people think as they actually do. It must help show how thoughts are produced and how they achieve, keep and lose the status of knowledge. It must shed light on how men behave, how their minds work and the nature of opinion, belief and judgment. It will do this only if it makes an attempt to show how mathematics is built up out of naturalistic components: experiences, psychological thought processes, natural pro‑pensities, habits, patterns of behaviour and institutions. To do this it is necessary to go beyond a study of the outcome of men's thinking. The task is to go behind the product to the acts of production themselves.

If there is going to be any real point in writing the history of mathematics in a way that is different from the great progressivist tradition it can only be because of the theoretical significance of the new questions that it can help to answer. The sociology of knowledge provides some of these new questions. It is these socio-psychological problems which the present chapters on mathematics have tried to bring into focus.

Returning to Lakatos's discussion of Euler's theorem: what under‑lying process does this bring to light? The answer is that it reveals a very important fact about mental and social processes. It shows that men

are not governed by their ideas or concepts. Even in mathematics, that
most cerebral of all subjects, it is men who govern ideas not ideas which
control men. The reason for this is simple. Ideas grow by having
something actively added to them. They are constructed and manu-
factured in order that they may be extended. These extensions of meaning and use do not pre-exist. The future uses and expanded meanings of
concepts, their entailments, are not present inside them in embryo.
Closer examination, reflection or analysis, cannot reveal the right or
wrong way to use a concept in a new situation. Notice that in Euler's
theorem the counter-examples and the proof-idea had to be actively
brought into contact with the concept of the polyhedron. In deciding what
was to count as a polyhedron there is no sense to be attached to saying
that the matter had already been decided by the meaning of the concept.
The meaning of the concept with regard to the counter-examples simply
did not exist. There was nothing lurking within the concept to constrain
men one way or the other. The concept of a polyhedron could not govern
men's behaviour in deciding what was to be included in, and what was to
be excluded from, its scope.

This does not mean that nothing acts as a constraint in these circumstances. The extension and elaboration of concepts can plausibly be seen
as both structured and determined. They are determined by the forces
at work in the situation of choice - forces which may be systematically
different for different men.

Take a simple example. A young child is taught the word 'hat' and
has learned to recognise some hats. He then notices a tea-pot lid and
calls it a hat. His extension of the concept is based on linking the new
particular case to the old particular cases. It is not mediated by any
abstract entity called the meaning of the concept hat. The link is via the
felt similarities and differences between the new object and the previous
cases. Parental authority will soon cut across the child's natural extension of the concept and insist that really the object is not a hat but a
lid. A socially sustained boundary is drawn across the flow of the psychological tendency. The child then sees a tea-cosy. Is it a lid or a hat?
The choice, which may be quite obvious, spontaneous and unreflective,
will be the outcome of the various response tendencies which converge on
the case. The older and perhaps stronger habit will compete with the
more novel restrictions. Should the tea-cosy bear an uncanny resembl-
ance to Mother's hats then this will no doubt clinch the case, until, that is,
the voice of authority draws another stern distinction.

In this simple learning situation it is not difficult to adopt a naturalistic stance and see the extension of the concepts emerging from the
factors operating on the child. It is easy to feel how past experience can
push this way and that. Nor is it hard to appreciate that extensions of
usage are not drawn towards any alleged, real meaning of the concepts.
Rather they are caused by diverse factors derived from past experience.
It should be possible to transfer this perspective to the data in Lakatos's
example. Of course that example did not bring out what caused the

diversity of judgment about what counts as a polyhedron.   This would be
a matter of examining the professional commitments and backgrounds of
the actors.   What it does show is the scope for the operation of these
factors.   It is in this sense that appreciating the creative role of
negotiation increases the need for a sociological perspective.   It removes
the myth that ideas lay down in advance the path which thinkers must
follow.   It removes the glib belief that the role of ideas in behaviour
excludes social factors as causes as if the two were in competition.

Chapter 8

CONCLUSION: WHERE DO WE STAND?

The categories of philosophical thought form an intellectual landscape.
Its great landmarks are named 'truth', 'objectivity', 'relativism',
'idealism', 'materialism', and so forth.   I shall conclude by taking my
bearings with respect to some of these landmarks and re-affirm which
ones identify the position that I have advocated.

Throughout the argument I have taken for granted and endorsed what
I think is the standpoint of most contemporary science.   In the main
science is causal, theoretical, value-neutral, often reductionist, to an
extent empiricist, and ultimately materialistic like common sense.   This
means that it is opposed to teleology, anthropomorphism and what is
transcendent.   The overall strategy has been to link the social sciences
as closely as possible with the methods of other empirical sciences.   In
a very orthodox way I have said: only proceed as the other sciences
proceed and all will be well.

In delineating the strong programme in the sociology of knowledge
I have tried to capture what I think sociologists actually do when they un-
self-consciously adopt the naturalistic stance of their discipline.   Danger
derives from shrinking from its full implications, not from pressing
forward.   It is only a partial view that will be prey to inconsistencies.   I
have selected a number of arguments which appear to pose the central
philosophical objections to the sociology of scientific knowledge.   Always
I have tried to respond not by retreat or compromise, but by elaborating
the basic standpoint of the social sciences.   Indeed the central themes of
this book, that ideas of knowledge are based on social images, that
logical necessity is a species of moral obligation, and that objectivity is
a social phenomenon, have all the characteristics of straightforward
scientific hypotheses.

The shortcomings of the views developed here are, no doubt, legion.
The one that I feel most keenly is that, whilst I have stressed the materialist character of the sociological approach, still the materialism tends to
be passive rather than active.   It cannot, I hope, be said to be totally un-
dialectical, but without doubt it represents knowledge as theory rather

than practice. The possibility for discovering the right blend seems to me to be there, even if it has not been realised. Nothing that has been said denies the technical power and sheer practicality of much of our knowledge, but its precise relation to theory remains a worry. For example, how do our manual skills relate to our consciousness? How different are the laws which govern these two things? The most that can be said in defence is that the critics of the sociology of knowledge rarely do any better. Indeed they appear to have less resources for coping with the problem than those with a naturalistic approach. It is salutary to remember that Popper's philosophy makes science a matter of pure theory rather than reliable technique. He only provides an ideology for the purest scientist and leaves the engineer and craftsman without succour.

Unfortunately the process of takings one's bearings, of finding where one stands, has its snags. Like the landscape through which John Bunyon's pilgrim progressed, the topography of the intellect is not morally neutral. The high Peaks of Truth glitter invitingly, but the foul Pit of Relativism will trap the unwary. Rationality and Causation struggle with one another as if they were the forces of Good and Evil. These stock responses and conventional evaluations are as inappropriate to the sociology of knowledge as they are predictable by it. Take relativism, for example. Philosophers sometimes perplex themselves because moral relativism seems philosophically acceptable but cognitive relativism does not. Their feelings are different in the two cases so they look for reasons to justify them. Scientifically, the same attitude towards both morality and cognition is possible and desirable. Relativism is simply the opposite of absolutism, and is surely preferable. In some forms it can at least be held authentically in the light of our social experience.

There is no denying that the strong programme in the sociology of knowledge rests on a form of relativism. It adopts what may be called 'methodological relativism', a position summarised in the symmetry and reflexivity requirements that were defined earlier. All beliefs are to be explained in the same way regardless of how they are evaluated.

One way in which the sociology of knowledge might polemically justify itself in its relativism is to insist that it is neither more nor less guilty than other conceptions of knowledge which usually escape the charge. Who charges Popper's theory with relativism? Indeed, when this charge is pressed against the sociology of knowledge doesn't it frequently come from those who are impressed by that philosophy? And yet the sociology of knowledge can easily formulate the essentials of its own standpoint in the terms of that philosophy. All knowledge, the sociologist could say, is conjectural and theoretical. Nothing is absolute and final. Therefore all knowledge is relative to the local situation of the thinkers who produce it: the ideas and conjectures that they are capable of producing; the problems that bother them; the interplay of assumption and criticism in their milieu; their purposes and aims; the experiences they have and the standards and meanings they apply.   What are all these factors other than naturalistic determinants of belief which can be studied sociologically and psychologically?   Nor is the situation altered because explaining behaviour and belief sometimes involves making assumptions about the physical world which surrounds the actors.   This only means that conjectures from say, physics or astronomy are used as subsidiary hypotheses.   If Popper is right this knowledge is conjectural too.   The whole of the explanation is a conjecture, albeit a conjecture about other conjectures.

Similarly a sociologist can embrace Popper's insistence that what makes knowledge scientific is not the truth of its conclusions but the procedural rules, standards and intellectual conventions to which it conforms. To say that knowledge is a question of standards and conventions is but to say it is a question of norms.   A conventionalist theory of knowledge such. as Popper's can be looked on as the abstract skeleton of a more realistic sociological account of knowledge.

To see all knowledge as conjectural and fallible is really the most extreme form of philosophical relativism.   But Popper is surely right to believe that we can have knowledge, and scientific knowledge, that is nothing but conjecture.   What constitutes the very existence of science is its status as an ongoing activity.   It is ultimately a pattern of thought and behaviour, a style of going about things which has its characteristic norms and values.   It does not need any ultimate metaphysical sanction to support it or make it possible.   There need be no such thing as Truth, other than conjectural, relative truth, any more than there need be absolute moral standards rather than locally accepted ones.   If we can live with moral relativism we can live with cognitive relativism.

Science may be able to work without absolute truth, but, such a thing might still exist.   This residual feeling surely rests on a confusion between truth and the material world.   It is the external, material world that really seems to be in mind when it is insisted that there must be some permanent truth.   This instinct seems unassailable.   But to believe in a material world does not justify the conclusion that there is any final or privileged state of adaptation to it which constitutes absolute knowledge or truth.   As Kuhn has argued with great clarity scientific progress - which is real enough - is like Darwinian evolution.   There is no goal for adaptation.   No meaning can be given to the idea of perfect or final adaptation. We have reached the present position in the progress and evolution of our knowledge, as we have in the evolution of our species, with no beacon to guide us, nor any goal.

Just as the sociology of knowledge is accused of relativism, as if it were a crime rather than a necessity, so it will be accused of subjectivism. Where does the sociology of knowledge stand with regard to the Rock of Objectivity?   Does it say that truly objective knowledge is impossible? Emphatically it does not.   What was proposed in the discussion of Frege, for example, was a sociological theory of objectivity.   If objectivity had been held to be non-existent there would have been no need to develop a

theory to account for it.   Nor is this a way of saying that objectivity is
an illusion.   It is real but its nature is totally different from what may
have been expected.   It is other theories of objectivity which are denied
by a sociological account, not the phenomenon itself.   Those who elect to
be champions of scientific objectivity might reflect on the following: a
sociological theory probably accords objectivity a more prominent role in
human life than they do.   On this theory moral knowledge can be objective
too.   Like many features of a landscape, knowledge looks different from
different angles.   Approach it from an unexpected route, glimpse it from
an unusual vantage point, and at first it may not be recognisable.

No doubt I will be exposed to the further charge of 'scientism', that
is, an over-optimistic belief in the power and progress of science.
Amusingly this criticism will have to stand shoulder to shoulder with
another charge, which has been examined at length: that this scientistic
approach, when practised by the sociology of knowledge and applied to
science itself, is a denigration of science.   I have given reasons why this
contradiction should be laid at the door of the critics rather than the strong
programme.   Nevertheless the charge of scientism is well aimed.   I am
more than happy to see sociology resting on the same foundations and
assumptions as other sciences.   This applies whatever their status and
origin.   Really sociology has no choice but to rest on these foundations,
nor any more appropriate model to adopt.   For that foundation is our
culture.   Science is our form of knowledge.   That the sociology of knowledge stands or falls with the other sciences seems to me both eminently
desirable as a fate, and highly probably as a prediction.

BIBLIOGRAPHY

BARBER, B. (1961), Resistance by scientists to scientific discovery, 'Science', vol. 134, no. 3479, pp. 596-602.

BARBER, B. and FOX, R. (1958), The case of the floppy-eared rabbits, 'American Journal of Sociology', no. 64, pp. 128-36.

BARKER, S. (1964), 'Philosophy of Mathematics', Prentice-Hall, Englewood Cliffs, N.J.

BARNES, B. (1974), 'Scientific Knowledge and Sociological Theory', Routledge & Kegan Paul, London.

BARTLETT, F.C. (1932), 'Remembering', Cambridge University Press, Cambridge.

BEN-DAVID, J. (1971), 'The Scientist's Role in Society', Prentice-Hall, Englewood Cliffs, N.J.

BLOOR, D. (1971), Two paradigms for scientific knowledge? 'Science Studies', vol. 1, no. 1, pp. 101-15.

BLOOR, D. (1973), Wittgenstein and Mannheim on the sociology of mathematics, 'Studies in the History and Philosophy of Science', vol. 4, no. 2, pp. 173-91.

BLOOR, D. (1974), Popper's mystification of objective knowledge, 'Science Studies', vol. 4, pp. 65-76.

BLOOR, D. (1975), Psychology or epistemology?, 'Studies in the History and Philosophy of Science', vol. 5, no. 4, pp. 382-95.

BOSANQUET, B. (1899), 'The Philosophical Theory of The State', Macmillan, London.

BOSTOCK, D. (1974), 'Logic and Arithmetic', Clarendon Press, Oxford.

BOTTOMORE, T.B. (1956), Some reflections on the sociology of knowledge, 'British Journal of Sociology', vol. 7, no. 1, pp. 52-8.

BOYER, C.B. (1959), 'The History of the Calculus and its Conceptual Development', Dover Publications, New York.

BRADLEY, F.H. (1876), 'Ethical Studies', Clarendon Press, Oxford.

BURCHFIELD, J.D. (1975), 'Lord Kelvin and the Age of the Earth', Macmillan, London.

BURKE, E. (1790), 'Reflections on the Revolution in France' in 'The Works of the Right Honourable Edmund Burke', vol. V, Rivington, London, 1808.

CAJORI, F. (1919), 'A History of Mathematics', (2nd edn), Macmillan, New York.

CARDWELL, D.S.L. (1971), 'From Watt to Clausius', Heinemann, London.

CARRUCCIO, E. (1964), 'Mathematics and Logic in History and in Contemporary Thought', trans. I. Quigley, Faber & Faber, London.

CASSIRER, E. (1950), 'The Problem of Knowledge', trans. W.H. Woglom and C.W. Hendel, Yale University Press, New Haven.

COLEMAN, W. (1970), Bateson and chromosomes: conservative thought in science, 'Centaurus', vol. 15, no. 3-4, pp. 228-314.

CONANT, J.B. (1966), The overthrow of phlogiston theory, in Conant and Nash (eds), 'Harvard Case Histories in Experimental Science', Harvard University Press, Cambridge, Mass.

COWAN, R.S. (1972), Francis Galton's statistical ideas: the influence of eugenics, 'Isis', vol. 63, pp. 509-28.

DEDEKIND, R. (1901), 'Essays on the Theory of Numbers', trans. W.W. Berman, Dover Publications, New York (1963).

DE GRÉ, G. (1967), 'Science as a Social Institution', Random House, New York.

DIENES, Z.P. (1960), 'Building up Mathematics', Hutchinson, London.

DIENES, Z.P. (1964), 'The Power of Mathematics', Hutchinson, London.

DOUGLAS, Mary (1966), 'Purity and Danger: An Analysis of Concepts of Pollution and Taboo', Routledge & Kegan Paul, London.

DOUGLAS, Mary (1970), 'Natural Symbols', Barrie & Jenkins, London.

DURKHEIM, E. (1915), 'The Elementary Forms of the Religious Life', trans. by J.W. Swain, Allen & Unwin, London (quotations are from the 1961 Collier Books edn).

DURKHEIM, E. (1938), 'The Rules of Sociological Method', trans. of 8th edn by S.A. Soloway and J.H. Mueller, The Free Press, New York.

EVANS-PRITCHARD, E.E. (1937), 'Witchcraft, Oracles and Magic among the Azande', Clarendon Press, Oxford.

FORMAN, P. (1971), Weimar Culture, Causality, and Quantum Theory, 1918 - 1927: Adaptation by German Physicists and Mathematicians to a Hostile Intellectual Environment, in R. McCormmach, ed. 'Historical Studies in the Physical Sciences', vol. 3, pp. 1-115.

FREGE, G. (1959), 'The Foundations of Arithmetic', trans. by J.L. Austin, Blackwell, Oxford.

FRENCH, P. (1972), 'John Dee', Routledge & Kegan Paul, London.

GIDDENS, A. (1972), 'Emile Durkheim: Selected Writings', ed. with introduction by A. Giddens, Cambridge University Press, Cambridge.

GOOCH, G.P. (1948), 'Studies in German History', Longmans, London.

HALÉVY, E. (1928), 'The Growth of Philosophical Radicalism', trans by M. Morris, Faber & Faber, London.

HAMLYN, D.W. (1969), 'The Psychology of Perception', Routledge & Kegan Paul, London.

HANEY, L.H. (1911), 'History of Economic Thought', Macmillan, New York.

HEATH, Sir T. (1910), 'Diophantus of Alexandria: A Study in the History of Greek Algebra', CUP, Cambridge (2nd edn).

HEATH, Sir T. (1921), 'A History of Greek Mathematics', 2 vols., Clarendon Press, Oxford.

HESSE, Mary (1966), 'Models and Analogies in Science', University of Notre Dame Press, Notre Dame.

HESSE, Mary (1974), 'The Structure of Scientific Inference', Macmillan, London.

HOBHOUSE, L.T. (1918), 'The Metaphysical Theory of the State', Allen & Unwin, London.

JANIK, A. and TOULMIN, S. (1973), 'Wittgenstein's Vienna', Weidenfeld & Nicolson, London.

KANTOROWICZ, H. (1937), Savigny and the historical school of law, 'Law Quarterly Review', vol. 53, pp. 326-43.

KLEIN, J. (1968), 'Greek Mathematical Thought and the Origin of Algebra', trans. E. Brann, The MIT Press, Cambridge, Mass. (first published in 1934 and 1936).

KUHN, T.S. (1957), 'The Copernican Revolution', Harvard University Press, Cambridge, Mass.

KUHN, T.S. (1959), Energy conservation as an example of simultaneous discovery, in M. Clagett (ed) 'Critical Problems in the History of Science', University of Wisconsin Press, Madison.

KUHN, T.S. (1962a), The historical structure of scientific discovery, 'Science', vol. 136, pp. 760-4.

KUHN, T.S. (1962b), 'The Structure of Scientific Revolution', University of Chicago Press, Chicago.

LAKATOS, I. (1962), Infinite regress and the foundations of mathematics, 'Proceedings of the Aristotelian Society' supplementary vol. 36, pp. 155-84.

LAKATOS, I. (1963-4), Proofs and refutations, 'British Journal for the Philosophy of Science', vol. 14, pp. 1-25, 120-39, 221-43, 296-342.

LAKATOS, I. (1967), A renaissance of empiricism in the recent philosophy of mathematics, in I. Lakatos (ed.), 'Problems in the Philosophy of Mathematics', North-Holland Publishing Company, Amsterdam, pp. 199-220.

LAKATOS, I. (1971), History of science and its rational reconstructions, in Buck and Cohen (eds), 'Boston Studies', vol. 8, Reidel, Dordrecht.

LAKATOS, I. and MUSGRAVE, A. (eds) (1970), 'Criticism and the Growth of Knowledge', Cambridge University Press, Cambridge.

LANGMUIR, I. (1953), ed. 1968 by R.N. Hall, 'Pathological Science', General Electric R and D Centre Report no. 68-c-035, New York.

LOVEJOY, A.O. (1940), Reflections on the History of Ideas, 'Journal of the History of Ideas', vol. 1, no. 1, pp. 3-23.

LUKES, S. (1974), Relativism: cognitive and moral, 'Proceedings of the Aristotelian Society', supplementary vol. 48, pp. 165-89.

LUMNER, O. (1904), M. Blondlot's n-ray experiments, 'Nature', vol. 69, pp. 378-80.

MCDOUGALL, W.(1920), 'The Group Mind', Cambridge University Press, Cambridge.

MANDER, J. (1974), 'Our German Cousins: Anglo-Saxon Relations in the 19th and 20th centuries', John Murray, London.

MANNHEIM, K. (1936), 'Ideology and Utopia', (trans. with an introduction by L. Wirth and E. Shils), Routledge & Kegan Paul, London.

MANNHEIM, K. (1952), 'Essays on the Sociology of Knowledge', Routledge & Kegan Paul, London.

MANNHEIM, K. (1953), Conservative thought in K. Mannheim, 'Essays on Sociology and Social Psychology', Routledge & Kegan Paul, London.

MERTON, R.K. (1957), Priorities in scientific discoveries', 'American Sociological Review', vol. 22, no. 6, pp. 635-59.

MERTON, R.K. (1964), 'Social Theory and Social Structure' (revised and enlarged ed), Collier-Macmillan, London.

MILL, J.S. (1848), 'A System of Logic: Ratiocinative and Inductive', Longmans, London. (The quotations are from the 1959 impression of the eighth edition. All references are given by citing the Book, Chapter and Section Number.)

MONTMORENCY, J.E.G. de (1913), Friedrich Carl von Savigny, in Sir J. Macdowell and E. Mason (eds), 'Great Jurists of the World', John Murray, London.

MORRELL, J.B. (1972), The chemist breeders: the research schools of Liebig and Thomas Thomson, 'Ambix', vol. XIX, no. 1, pp. 1-46.

NASH, L.K. (1966), The atomic-molecular theory, in J.B. Conant and L.K. Nash (eds) 'Harvard Case Histories in Experimental Science', Harvard University Press, Cambridge, Mass.

NISBET, R.A. (1967), 'The Sociological Tradition', Heinemann, London.

PASCAL, R. (1939), Herder and the Scottish historical school, 'Publications of the English Goethe Society', New Series, vol. XIV, pp. 23-42.

PETERS, R.S. (1958), 'The Concept of Motivation', Routledge & Kegan Paul, London.

PIAGET, J. (1952), 'The Child's Concept of Number', trans. C. Cattegro and F.M. Hodgson, Routledge & Kegan Paul, London.

POINCARÉ, H. (1908), 'Science and Method', trans. F. Maitland, Dover Publications, New York, (n.d.).

POLYA, G. (1954), 'Analogy and Induction', vol. 1 of 'Mathematics and Plausible Reasoning', Princeton University Press, Princeton.

POPPER, K.R. (1959), 'The Logic of Scientific Discovery', Hutchinson, London (first published 1934).

POPPER, K.R. (1960), 'The Poverty of Historicism', Routledge & Kegan Paul, London.

POPPER, K.R. (1963), 'Conjectures and Refutations', Routledge & Kegan Paul, London.

POPPER, K.R. (1966), 'The Open Society and its Enemies', vol. 2, Routledge & Kegan Paul, London.
POPPER, K.R. (1972), 'Objective Knowledge', Clarendon Press, Oxford.
REISS, H.S. (1955), 'The Political Thought of the German Romantics, 1793-1815', Blackwell, Oxford.
RUDWICK, M.J.S. (1972), 'The Meaning of Fossils', Macdonald, London.
RUDWICK, M.J.S. (1974), Darwin and Glen Roy: a' great failure' in scientific method? 'Studies in the History and Philosophy of Science', vol. 5, no. 2, pp. 97-185.
RUSSELL, B.(1956), 'Portraits from Memory', Allen & Unwin, London.
RYLE, G. (1949), 'The Concept of Mind', Hutchinson, London.
SCHEFFLER, I. (1967), 'Science and Subjectivity', Bobbs-Merrill, New York.
SKINNER, B.F. (1945), The operational analysis of psychological terms, 'Psychological Review', vol. 52, pp. 270-7.
SPENGLER, O. (1926), 'The Decline of the West', trans. by C.F. Atkinson, Allen & Unwin, London.
STARK, W. (1941 and 46), Liberty and Equality or: Jeremy Bentham as an economist, 'Economic Journal', vol. 51, pp. 56-79, and vol. 56, pp. 583-608.
STARK, W. (1958),'The Sociology of Knowledge', Routledge & Kegan Paul, London.
STAUDE, J.R. (1967), 'Max Scheler, 1874-1928', The Free Press, New York, ch. 3, The genius of the war.
STORER, N.W. (1966), 'The Social System of Science', Holt, Rinehart & Winston, New York.
STRONG, E.W. (1966), 'Procedures and Metaphysics', Georg Olms, Hildersheim (first published 1936).
TOULMIN, S. (1957), Crucial experiments: Priestley and Lavoisier, 'Journal of the History of Ideas', vol. 18, pp. 205-20.
TURNER, R.S. (1971), The growth of professorial research in Prussia, 1818 to 1848 - Causes and Context, in R. McCormmach (ed), 'Historical Studies in the Physical Sciences', vol. 3, pp. 137-82.
VAN DER WAERDEN, B.L. (1954), 'Science Awakening', trans. A. Dresden, Noordhoff, Groningen.
WARRINGTON, J. (1956), translation of Aristotle's 'Metaphysics', Dent, London.
WATKINS, D.S. (1969), Blondlot's n-rays: a history of a notable scientific error, unpublished paper from Department of Liberal Studies, University of Manchester.
WILLIAMS, R. (1958), 'Culture and Society 1780-1950', Chatto & Windus, London.
WINCH, P. (1964), Understanding a primitive society, 'American Philosophical Quarterly', vol. 1, pp. 307-24.
WITTGENSTEIN, L. (1956), 'Remarks on the Foundations of Mathematics', Blackwell, Oxford.

WOLFF, K.H. (1964) (ed) 'Essays on Sociology and Philosophy by Emile Durkheim et al', Harper & Row, New York.

WOOD, R.W. (1904), The n-rays, 'Nature', vol. 70, pp. 530-1.

YATES, Frances, A. (1972), 'The Rosicrucian Enlightenment', Routledge & Kegan Paul, London.

YOUNG, R.M. (1969), Malthus and the evolutionists: the common context of biological and social theory, 'Past & Present', vol. 43, pp. 109-45.

ZNANIECKI, F. (1965), 'The Social Role of The Man of Knowledge', Octagon Books, New York.

INDEX